Walks For All Ages
Greater Manchester

WALKS *FOR* ALL *AGES*

GREATER MANCHESTER

NEIL COATES

BRADWELL
BOOKS

Published by Bradwell Books
9 Orgreave Close Sheffield S13 9NP
Email: books@bradwellbooks.co.uk

1st Edition 2014

Reprinted 2016

ISBN: 9781909914414

Print: Gomer Press, Llandysul, Ceredigion SA44 4JL

Design by: Erik Siewko Creative, Derbyshire.
eriksiewko@gmail.com

Photograph Credits: © Neil Coates

Maps: Contain Ordnance Survey data
© Crown copyright and database right 2014

Ordnance Survey licence number 100039353

The information in this book has been produced in good faith and is intended as a general guide. Bradwell Books and its authors have made all reasonable efforts to ensure that the details are correct at the time of publication. Bradwell Books and the author cannot accept any responsibility for any changes that have taken place subsequent to the book being published.

It is the responsibility of individuals undertaking any of the walks listed in this publication to exercise due care and consideration for the health and wellbeing of each other in the party. Particular care should be taken if you are inexperienced. The walks in this book are not especially strenuous but individuals taking part should ensure they are fit and able to complete the walk before setting off.

INTRODUCTION

Welcome to Walks for all Ages Greater Manchester. With magnificent moors and intriguing heritage; wooded gorges and tranquil vales; peaceful farmland and moody lakes, the jigsaw of landscapes in Greater Manchester is endlessly fascinating.

Centred on Manchester, Greater Manchester county was created in the early 1970s from parts of Lancashire, Cheshire and the West Riding of Yorkshire. Cotton towns like Bolton and Oldham were included; as were Cheshire spinning towns such as Hyde and Stockport. Much less obvious are the areas of countryside that were integrated into the new county. From the low ridges fringing Wigan to the heather-clad heights of the West Pennines; from the great edges of the Dark Peak to the stone villages of the South Pennines; and in the woods and pasturelands of the river valleys, an extremely varied terrain awaits discovery.

The 20 walks featured here explore every sort of landscape; they're real country rambles, not sanitised strolls. None are difficult or very steep, but most include hills, some short and sharp; some are uneven underfoot and have steps or gates. The walks largely avoid stiles, but several routes across farmland do include some; cattle and sheep may well be encountered. The walks are between 2 and 5½ miles long. In general they follow well-marked and used lanes, paths, towpaths and tracks – and can be muddy! Please dress sensibly and be aware of your own safety and capabilities.

Most of the walks are accessible by local bus, train or tram services; information is included at the start of each chapter, or you can visit the Transport for Greater Manchester (TfGM) website (www.tfgm.com) or ring Traveline (0871 200 2233) for more information. A short hop away from the crowded town centres is another England just waiting to be discovered and enjoyed.

I hope that the walks I've chosen will prove a pleasant introduction to the great pastime of rambling in this most enticing, varied and underestimated part of the realm.

Easy walking in the miniature lakeland between Leigh & Wigan where one of England's premier birdwatching spots marks the site of long-gone collieries.

There's not much left of the once-vast Lancashire coalfield. Here and there remnants of spoil-tips still form miniature areas of hills, whilst the occasional pit-head winding gear and buildings are preserved. The most obvious remains are probably the latticework of old railways that still thread between towns, villages and the main lines; overgrown and lost highways of the industrial era. But there are significant features dotting the landscape which are rarely associated with the old pits.

These are the lodges and flashes which occur all over the former coalfield. The lodges are generally small-scale water features used to store water for use in colliery boiler systems; the flashes, however, are inspiring places to visit, and the grand-daddy of them all is Pennington Flash, just outside Leigh. It's the largest of a strand of reedy mosses and areas of open water stretching up towards Wigan, where the renowned Wigan Flashes temper the post-industrial landscape.

Pennington's enormous lake is not natural, but first formed just over a century ago in a depression in the land surface caused by the collapse of underground coal workings. The extent of those workings can be gauged from the size of the lake, which is about 175 acres in extent. Two farms once stood where the water is; their fields were abandoned in the early 1900s due to the worsening flooding by local brooks, which eventually filled the flash. It's not very deep and occasionally all-but dried out between the wars. In the 1960s banking was created to ensure a continual presence of water, and the lake was managed as a flood-control reservoir.

Recreational use began after the Second War when a yachting club was formed here, and it has been a country park since 1981. It's now one of the foremost birdwatching centres of northern England, with a series of hides around the shoreline. Over 230 different species have been noted here, with rarities like marsh harriers, spoonbills and water rails the cream of the crop.

This walk is a circuit of the lake, added to which a section of the towpath of the Leeds & Liverpool Canal is followed, widening the views. This opened in 1820 and meets head-on in Leigh with the earlier Bridgewater Canal from Worsley and Manchester, connecting the isolated Leeds & Liverpool with the national waterways network.

THE BASICS

Distance: 3¼ miles / 5.25km
Gradient: Virtually level throughout
Severity: Easy
Approximate time: 2 hrs
Stiles: Two
Map: OS Explorer 276 (Bolton, Wigan and Warrington)
Path description: Sandy and surfaced paths; earth tracks; towpath; pavements
Start point: Aspull Common (GR: SJ 644985)
Parking: Car park along Flash entry road opposite Robin Hood pub (WN7 3PA)
Dog friendly: On leads as appropriate
Public toilets: At the Information Centre
Nearest refreshment: The Robin Hood pub, opposite Country Park entrance
Public transport: Frequent buses on the 600 Leigh to Wigan route pass the Robin Hood at Aspull Common (Tel: Traveline 0871 200 2233)

1. From the car park entrance turn left; then in 50 yards left again on a tarred way past a gate. In another 120 yards go right on a path alongside trees, soon reaching a junction. Go ahead to join the waterside path around the Flash, turning right here. You'll soon reach the first of the bird hides that dot the shoreline, where you'll often find enthusiasts keen to tell of the birds currently here. The path curls to the head of an inlet; cross into the car park and continue to the far end and Information Centre.

2. Keep the Flash immediately on your left. The path shortly cuts through an area of scrapes, ponds and islets, amidst which are further bird

    hides. Stay on the main path, passing Tom Edmondson's hide, to a multi-route junction in 250 yards; here rise to the nearby canal towpath. Turn left and walk to the substantial Plank Lane lift bridge. The new marina moorings on the far bank mark the edge of the Bickershaw Colliery complex, the last of Lancashire's deep pits, which closed in 1992. Way behind, on the horizon is Winter Hill ridge, the highest land in the West Pennine Moors.

3. Turn down the road, pass the car park and continue to the right-hand bend. Look carefully on the left for a narrow dirt path (not the ones by a barrier, but 50 yards further on) which shortly bends left, then crosses a flat bridge. Stick on this path to skirt past Mossley Hall Farm to the main road. Cross; then turn left and bend right into Sandy Lane. In 100 yards turn left along Green Lane, beside the sailing club entrance.

4. Continue past terraced cottages and then through the complex at Sorrowcow Farm, remaining on the waymarked track beyond the buildings. Some 100 yards beyond a flat bridge, fork left twice to regain the shoreline path in 200 yards. Go right with it. In 140 yards drop left down a few steps; in another 100 yards fork right at benches. Cross the cross-path; in a few yards turn sharp right and walk to a T-junction in 120 yards. Go left to the access road, then right to the car park.

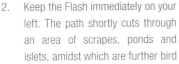

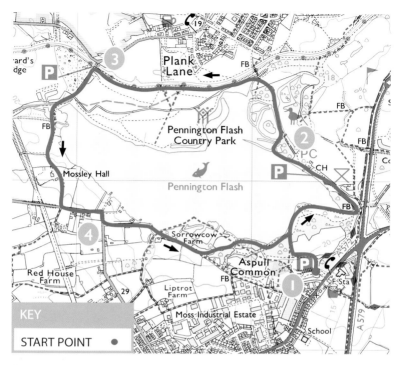

KEY

START POINT ●

Better to start at ② ○ car park/toilets.

DUNHAM MASSEY

STROLL BESIDE ONE OF ENGLAND'S FIRST CANALS; DISCOVER TRANQUIL VILLAGE INNS AND SPOT FALLOW DEER ON A HUGE COUNTRY ESTATE AT THE FRINGE OF THE MERSEY VALLEY.

Cheshire is littered with vast country estates. This easy ramble straddles the boundary of Cheshire and Greater Manchester and explores an estate that can trace its origins back to the time of William the Conqueror. It also follows one of the oldest canals in the country.

A huge deer park surrounds the great house at Dunham Massey. The herd of fallow deer here is used to visitors and the animals are usually very easy to see. If you're accompanied by a dog then keep it on a very tight lead anywhere within the estate.

The walk starts from the main car park and first skirts the parkland boundary, reaching the bank of the River Bollin beside an eye-catching Georgian corn mill, now redeveloped as apartments. Crossing below the mill-weir, the route threads through the tranquil hamlet of Little Bollington, largely built to house workers from the Dunham Massey estate. There's a handy pub here for an early rest break.

A byroad slips from the little green to pass beneath an aqueduct. This carries the Bridgewater Canal high above the shallow valley of the Bollin, and is rightly renowned as one of the wonders of Britain's inland waterways. The vast, curving embankment was originally built in the 1770s by the famous engineer James Brindley. It is part of the system of canals financed by the Duke of Bridgewater to transport coal from his mines to the growing cities of Liverpool and Manchester. It's generally recognised as the first major canal built in Britain since Roman times.

An easy towpath ramble gives views across the Dunham estate. After one mile the canal is left behind as the route passes through another of the estate villages, Dunham Town, to reach the two-mile-long deer park wall at Charcoal Lodge. The approach to the Hall is a bold avenue of trees, many around 300 years old and some even older. The current

hall, passed to the National Trust in 1976 by the last Earl of Stamford, is a sturdy Georgian building built on the site of the original moated Norman manor. Nearby is a fairytale old watermill that latterly served as the estate sawmill; the machinery is still regularly run.

NB. The car park is open 9am to 7.30pm March to October; 9am to 5pm November to February.

THE BASICS

Distance: 3½ miles / 5.75km

Gradient: Mostly flat; one easy flight of steps up to canal

Severity: Easy

Approximate time: 2¼ hrs

Stiles: Five

Map: OS Explorer 276 (Bolton, Wigan and Warrington)

Path description: Tarred roads, byways and paths, towpath

Start point: National Trust car park, Dunham Massey Hall (GR: SJ 732875)

Parking: Dunham Massey Estate main National Trust car park (fee) (WA14 4SJ)

Dog friendly: On short leads in deer park; long leads elsewhere

Public toilets: Facilities at Dunham Massey Hall estate yard

Nearest refreshment: Cafe and restaurant at Dunham Massey Hall; tearoom at Little Bollington; two pubs along the way

Public transport: Bus 5 between Altrincham and Warrington passes Dunham Massey car park entrance (Tel: Traveline 0871 200 2233)

DUNHAM MASSEY WALK

1. From the car park entrance/exit turn left along the road, then left again along the gated wall-side lane for Bollington Mill (ignore the 'Private' sign; it is a public path). At the mill turn right and cross the footbridge over the River Bollin to find the inn at Little Bollington. Continue another 100 yards to the small green, where a lane diverges to the right. Follow this to reach the embankment carrying the canal.

2. Pass under this and take the stepped path, right, up to the towpath. Turn left and remain with it for the next mile (1.5km), presently crossing the aqueduct above the River Bollin far below.

3. Just before the second brick overbridge leave the towpath via the railed path and cross the bridge. You'll soon pass The Axe & Cleaver pub before reaching tiny Dunham Town at St Mark's Church. Just past the village shop be alert for the path on the left, which doglegs behind the white cottage to become a hedged way past the burial ground.

4. In about 175 yards, as the hedgerow turns left, go right to reach a stile onto the narrow Oldfield Lane. Walk right 20 yards to the corner; here slip left by the stile onto the hedge-side path to reach a crossing track in 100 yards. Turn left to reach a stile onto the golf course. Head half-right on the well-walked path, passing the brick hut to find the 12th tee (left). Here; turn back-right (iron signboard here) across the fairway to woodland at the far side; then continue through the copse to reach the main road opposite Charcoal Lodge.

5. Carefully cross to the main driveway to Dunham Massey Hall, climbing a low ladder-stile into the parkland. Remain with the tree-lined driveway to pass the front of the Hall. Go straight ahead and you will find the old watermill just to the left of the stables complex. Turn right from the watermill and walk the tarred track beside the moat with the pond to the Visitor Centre and car park.

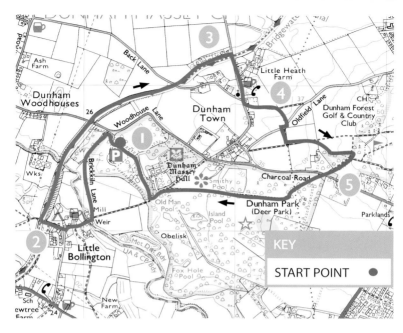

KEY

START POINT ●

WORSLEY WOODS

This is an easy walk in the area where the Industrial Revolution really took off, combining canal towpath, old railway and some superb woodland.

Whilst Worsley is renowned for its industrial heritage, the clock can be wound back another 2,000 years. Workmen digging on nearby Chat Moss in the late 1950s unearthed a severed head. It was feared a murder had been revealed. Tests later proved that the head, remarkably preserved by the 'pickling' effect of the peat, dated from the Iron Age. The head of 'Worsley Man' is in Manchester Museum's collection.

The Third Duke of Bridgewater, Francis Egerton, put Worsley on the map. Seeing the potential of the new-fangled transport innovation, the canal, he met with engineer James Brindley in 1759. The Duke's coalfield beneath his lands at Worsley was restricted by the limitations of using packhorses and wagons to transport the coal to the new markets in Manchester. By developing a canal to move the fuel production and profits could be hugely increased. Thus was born the Bridgewater Canal, which reached Manchester by 1765.

This easy stroll around the environs of Worsley discovers the heart of this network of waterways, many of which were underground. Along the way are picturesque mock-Tudor buildings, old cottages and a surprising countryside by the M60 motorway. At Worsley Delph the entrance to the mine canal system is visible, whilst at Worsley Green are tantalising reminders of the Georgian and Victorian complexes that made the Duke and his ancestors a huge fortune. The leafy canalside stroll then gives way to a ramble along the trackbed of one of the many railways that criss-crossed Salford until the 1960's. Now a wildlife-rich corridor, it leads to paths through Worsley Woods, one of the oldest areas of ancient woodland in Greater Manchester, rich with bluebells, ramsons and many other spring wildflowers.

From pretty Beesley Green, with its trim cricket ground and picket-fenced cottages, wildflower and local interest trails thread the woods. Our ramble slinks alongside the Kempnough Brook, ending up beside Old Warke Dam, created in the 1850's as fishing and hunting reserve for the First Earl of Ellesmere. From here it's a short stroll to Worsley with its pub, tearooms and the picturesque Court House, built by the First Earl as the Manorial Court for Worsley in 1849.

THE BASICS

Distance: 4½ miles / 7.25km
Gradient: Largely level
Severity: Easy
Approximate time: 2½ hrs
Stiles: None
Map: OS Explorer 276 (Bolton, Wigan and Warrington) & 277 (Manchester and Salford)
Path description: Firm towpath, compacted tracks, woodland paths; muddy in places
Start point: Worsley Court House (GR: SD 747004)
Parking: Car park (fee) beside Barton Road, opposite Worsley Court House (M28 2PB)
Dog friendly: On leads as appropriate
Public toilets: None
Nearest refreshment: Tearooms, pub and restaurants in Worsley & Parrin Lane Bridge
Public transport: Many buses to Worsley from Salford, Manchester, Bolton and other towns (Tel: Traveline 0871 200 2233)

WORSLEY WOODS WALK

1. Cross from the car park and turn left, then right past the Court House along Worsley Road. Cross at the bus stop to view The Delph; this ochre-coloured pool is the canal arm from the main canal to the entrance to the underground workings. Village interpretation boards fill in the story of this historic area. Continue along Worsley Road, crossing back over again in 100 yards to The Green. Near the brick monument across the green, cross the cobbled bridge over the Bridgewater Canal and turn left on the towpath, canal on your left. This is the route for the next mile (1.5km). Much redevelopment has swept away the busy wharves and waterside business of old. The tree-lined towpath eventually reaches a massive cast-iron road overbridge at Parrin Lane.

2. Rise onto the bridge, cross it (note the lighthouse in the trees on your right!) and in another 50 yards turn left up the rising, railed path which then joins the line of the old railway. This forges a way between Worsley Golf Club and Broad Oak Park, both important sanctuaries for wild birds and animals. Beyond an overbridge the woods thicken up; presently the walk passes beneath the noisy M60 motorway. Just before the next overbridge at Greenleach Lane (about 400 yards, where the line forks) go up the steps on your right.

3. Turn left over the bridge. In another 100 yards turn left onto Beesley Green. Fork right; then in 50 yards swing right with the footpath towards the woods. Keep left behind the buildings; the path then runs beside the shallow Kempnough Brook into Worsley Woods. Follow signs for Old Warke Dam before passing beneath the M60 again.

4. Now keep ahead on the main path to reach Old Warke Dam pool. Put this on your right and walk the fenced path to and past the dam (not over it) to a tarred lane. Advance to the main road. Look opposite-right for the footpath beside the red telephone box, which cuts (via a footbridge) in front of the attractive Packet House, from where passenger flyboats to Manchester ran from the 1770s. Beyond; cross the main road to the car park.

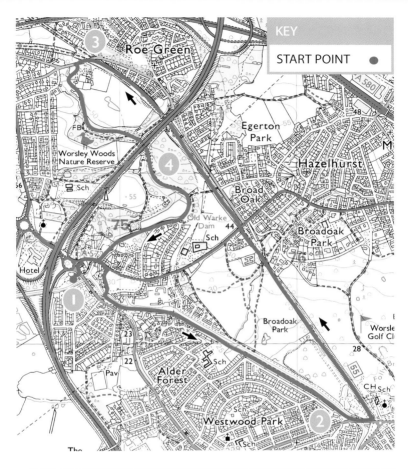

KEY

START POINT ●

HAUGHTON DALE

A TRANQUIL WALK COMBINING CANAL TOWPATH AND RIVERSIDE TRACKS IN THE WOODED VALLEY OF THE RIVER TAME WHERE THE GHOSTS OF INDUSTRY STILL TANTALISE AND WILDLIFE THRIVES.

Woodley, at the heart of suburban Stockport, fringes some absorbing countryside. Just to the east of the centre a splinter of gritstone moorland stretches out from the Dark Peak. Along the summit of this hilly ridge is Werneth Low Country Park, a popular area with active locals. Immediately north of the centre is the more gentle valley of the River Tame; it's here that this walk heads, visiting secluded woodlands and industrial heritage on an easy ramble largely along towpath and sandy tracks.

It's a great area for wildlife, with woodpeckers, jays and nuthatches in the magnificent beech woods; buzzards floating overhead and the paths, tracks and woods bright with foxgloves, wild garlic, bluebells and dog's mercury. The Tame rises on the moors 15 miles to the north, close to the summit of White Hill, high above the M62 motorway. This is on England's great watershed; rivers flow from this either west towards the Irish Sea or east to the North Sea. The Tame heads for Liverpool Bay, via the River Mersey from central Stockport.

The walk first joins the towpath of the Lower Peak Forest Canal, beside the northern portal of Woodley Tunnel. A tree-lined section swiftly takes the route beyond housing and into sloping pastures, with woodland bubbling down to the Tame below. On the far canal bank is Unity Mills and wharf, now derelict but once a large cotton-spinning enterprise built in the 1860s. Nearby was the compact Hall Lane Colliery, opened in 1829 and for which the wharf was originally built.

Further along this lovely wooded section are scant remains of Gee Cross Mill, demolished in the 1990s. It's near here that the walk drops down to cross the River Tame below a thundering weir, built to help power the vast Gibraltar Mills' waterwheels and boilers between 1760 and 1967. Heading downstream into Haughton Dale nature reserve, today's peaceful hayfields and secluded terraces hide the fact that a huge wireworks, The Meadow Factory, stood here until 100 years ago.

Re-crossing the river over Arden Bridge; some way downstream are some large boulders. One, known as Robin Hood's Stone, was said to have been flung here from Werneth Low by the medieval bandit whilst in a rage.

NOTE: For **Public transport:** Frequent 330 buses to Woodley Precinct from Stockport and Hyde (Tel: Traveline 0871 200 2233)

THE BASICS

Distance: 3¾ miles / 6km

Gradient: Mostly level with one gradual climb near end

Severity: Easy

Approximate time: 2 hrs

Stiles: None

Map: OS Explorer 277 (Manchester and Salford)

Path description: Canal towpath, sandy tracks and paths, woodland paths, tarred roads; muddy in places

Start point: Woodley Precinct (GR: SJ 932920)

Parking: Woodley Precinct (free) (SK6 1RJ)

Dog friendly: On long leads as necessary

Nearest refreshment: Cafes and pubs in Woodley

HAUGHTON DALE WALK

1. At Woodley Precinct put the Woodley Arms on your left and walk to the Methodist Church in 300 yards; slip down the cobbled path on your left and join the towpath, canal on your right. Remain with it for one mile (1.5km); a beautiful stretch soon gilded by fragrant hawthorns and shaded by superb beech woods. Stay on the towpath until you can see footbridge No. 8A, a metal lattice footbridge, about 100 yards ahead. On your right here is a modern house built on the site of Gee Cross Mill; the stone wharfing stones remain as the canal bank.

2. At this point leave the towpath to walk down the waymarked walled path – the cobbles may be slippery in wet weather – dropping to an old lane. Keep downhill to a wide bridge across the River Tame a few yards downstream of a weir. This is where the huge Gibraltar Mill once stood. Cross the bridge and turn downstream towards Hulme's Wood, soon keeping left along the riverbank path. Past a river bend this rejoins the wider path up a few steps. Keep downstream and favour the riverside path rather than the lane

in front of cottages. The butterfly-rich meadows here were the site of Meadow Mill cotton-spinning mill, then a wire works; all that remain are the powerful weir and a few reedy watercourses. This path presently bends right, away from the river, skirting a copse to reach the end of a rough lane.

3. Turn up past bungalows to the point where tarmac begins at a row of cottages. Turn left through the barrier here on a wide track waymarked Stockport Road. Keep ahead below the woods to reach the riverbank once again at Arden footbridge.

4. Cross this and turn left along the rough lane to reach a junction just past a barrier. Fork left to the entrance to the kennels' driveway. Pick up the parallel fenced path here (can be muddy); at the end of the buildings the path bends right to rise up widely spaced steps through the woods to regain the canal towpath. Turn right back to Woodley Tunnel portal; slip up and right here to return to the start along the main road.

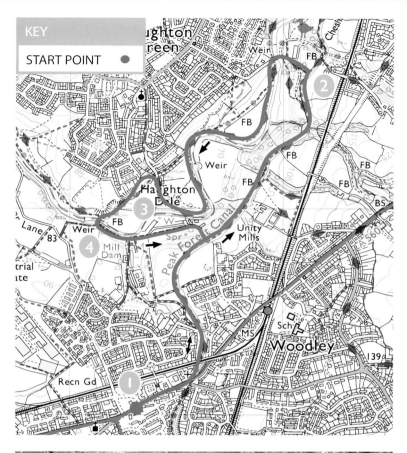

KEY

START POINT ●

HAIGH HALL

A WOODED STROLL WITH HIDDEN DEPTHS AND HERITAGE ON A CIRCUIT OF CANAL, VALLEY AND LANDSCAPED PARKLAND SURROUNDING ONE OF WIGAN'S GREAT COUNTRY HOUSES.

The country park surrounding Haigh Hall is one of Wigan's green lungs; a chance to escape the town for a countryside treat. Much of this walk is along back lanes and tracks; generally good underfoot with just a few slopes and steps to conquer. Lanes and byways that are largely traffic free string from the Hall's main car park through the golf course and down to the Leeds & Liverpool Canal. The way then falls gently down into the valley of the River Douglas, heading south to the hamlet of Leyland Mill Brow.

There's a little industry still here today, but the former ironworks is long gone. This was part of the industrial empire of the Earls of Crawford and Balcarres who lived at Haigh Hall. Coal and iron made them a vast fortune in the Georgian and Victorian ages. It's believed that Britain's largest waterwheel, the Lady Isabella at Laxey on the Isle of Man, was cast here at Haigh furnaces. It was made in sections before being moved by 'road locomotive' and canal from this riverside foundry to Liverpool's docks, from where it was shipped to the island in 1851.

There's a shallow climb back out of the valley to the parkland surrounding Haigh Hall. Much of this is covered in superb natural woodland; other parts are broadleaf plantations made on the order of the Earls. The plantations and 'rides' (roads) were created to help relieve great poverty being suffered by locals made redundant from the cotton mills of the area during the American Civil War, when no cotton could be exported from the great east coast ports of the southern states. Without raw material, the Lancashire cotton mills couldn't function; planting woodland was a Victorian job-creation scheme – and it also sheltered the Hall from the sight and sound of the collieries and ironworks!

Crossing an old mineral railway and visiting the canal, the walk drifts through woods and past the Swan Pond. There may be swans here, but the name comes from swan mussels, a large freshwater shellfish that was grown here for consumption at the Earls' table. The mansion at Haigh, reached at the end of the walk, was built in the 1830s, and is now owned by Wigan Council and used as a conference centre and wedding venue.

THE BASICS

Distance: 4 miles / 6.5km

Gradient: Mostly gentle ascents and descents; a few steps

Severity: Easy

Approximate time: 2½ hrs

Stiles: None

Map: OS Explorer 276 (Bolton, Wigan and Warrington)

Path description: Tarred lanes, farm tracks, woodland paths, towpath; possibly muddy in places

Start point: Haigh Hall, Copperas Lane, Wigan (GR: SD 596087)

Parking: Main car park, Haigh Hall (pay & display) (WN2 1PE)

Dog friendly: On leads

Public toilets: At start

Nearest refreshment: Café at start

HAIGH HALL WALK

1. From the car park exit go left on the road. In 200 yards turn left down the narrow lane between railings. This, Sennicar Lane, drops as a deep hollow-way through a copse and past cottages before crossing the canal. Remain on the lane to its end and a junction in the valley well past Rothwells Stud Farm.

2. Bear left along Wingates Road, threading through sturdy woodland above the River Douglas before rising to a junction at a mini-roundabout at Leyland Mill Brow. The factory buildings here are on the site of the Haigh furnace.

3. Turn left, slip up the cobbled path cutting the corner and carry on up the lane another 250 yards to find a fingerposted driveway on the right just beyond Rose Cottage. Turn along this; at the bend by the elegant old house slip left on the path down into the woods. At the stone Wigan Way marker, turn left on a wider track which curls round to a major junction. Turn left to cross an old railway bridge. Stick with the good track ahead, one of the old drives to the Hall, rising easily through the woods to reach a canal bridge. (No. 60)

4. Turn right onto the towpath of the Leeds & Liverpool Canal, with the water on your left. This is the main line of England's longest canal; here a long, nine-mile (15km) 'pound' (a stretch without locks) between Wigan Top Lock and Whittle-le-Woods. Cross at the next footbridge (No. 59B) and turn left on the tarred path. About 50 yards beyond the metal hand gate, fork right on the good path within the woods; keeping a field off to your right, then continue up a wooded sleeve between fields. Curve left to Mowpin Lodge cottage.

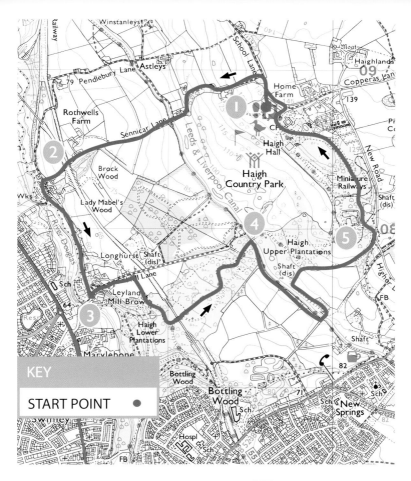

KEY

START POINT •

5. Choose the track left of the building, shortly bending left to find a wider track just beyond the miniature railway. Turn right, soon passing by the Swan Pond, then re-cross the railway before eventually emerging from the trees beside a crazy golf course. Continue left to reach Haigh Hall stables and the nearby car park.

RAMBLE ROUND A RESERVOIR VIA WOODED CLOUGHS AND A HISTORIC VILLAGE NESTLED IN THE DEEP VALLEY OF ONE OF THE WEST PENNINES' VIGOROUS LITTLE RIVERS.

The area to the north of Bolton is often called Lancashire's Lake District. The arc of moors that forms the horizon here is dotted by lakes. Nowadays these reservoirs are a source of drinking water, but the origin of many of them is quite different.

In the days before the Industrial Revolution, small-scale weaving and spinning enterprises developed. Hand and foot-operated looms were used to produce small amounts of cloth, bringing in valuable extra money to poor farming households. The distinctive gallery-style mullioned windows seen across the top storeys of older houses mark these out as former locations for weaving.

As demand increased, larger mills were required; powered first by waterwheels, then steam engines. Watercourses like Bradshaw Brook were dammed to store water, both to power the mills and to provide a basic water supply for the workers and towns. This was the origin of the reservoirs at Turton & Entwistle (built 1832) and Wayoh (1876), north of Turton Bottoms. This pretty village is visited on this walk, where remains of old Victorian mills haunt the valley floor and the flanks of Bradshaw Brook.

On the hillside above the village rises the 140 feet (43m) high old mill stack known as Old Russia Lodge chimney, remnant of the Quarlton Vale Print and Bleach Works. Black Rock bleachworks; Spinningside spinning mill, Vale and Stone Mills all harnessed the power of the brooks and all are now memories, whilst Horrobin bleachworks once stood where Jumbles Reservoir now glistens and reflects the surrounding woodland.

Jumbles Reservoir was created in 1971 to improve the water supply to Bolton, and guarantee that the rivers lower down didn't run dry. It's now a popular recreational facility, with thriving sailing and angling clubs and peaceful footpaths circling it. This walk makes the most of this, combining easy waterside strolling with a little exploration of

the older heritage of the area, rising just high enough out of the valley to reveal glorious views across farmland to the surrounding moors.

If you have time, it's worth visiting Turton Tower, just west of Jumbles Reservoir beside the B6391. This remarkable building is, in parts, over 800 years old. It was home to the wealthy Kay family, textile magnates of the Victorian era, and has fine paintings, furniture and lots of oddities.

NOTE: For Public transport: Bus 273 Bolton to Rawtenstall passes The Visitor Centre approach road. Bus 537 Bolton to Edgworth serves Turton Bottoms (Tel: Traveline 0871 200 2233)

THE BASICS

Distance: 2 miles / 3km or 3½ miles / 5.5km
Gradient: One gradual, short climb; another climb on longer route
Severity: Easy
Approximate time: 1½ or 2½ hrs
Stiles: Five
Map: OS Explorer: 287 (West Pennine Moors)
Path description: Field paths, stony tracks, lanes; muddy in places; long grass in section 4; cattle possible in section 5 & 6
Start point: Jumbles Countryside Centre, Bradshaw Road, Bolton (GR: SD 736140)
Parking: Jumbles Countryside Centre Car Park (pay & display) (BL2 4JS)
Dog friendly: On leads where appropriate
Public toilets: At start
Nearest refreshment: Café at start; pubs in Edgworth, north of Turton Bottoms

JUMBLES WALK

1. From the back corner of the car park a path and steps drop to a footbridge below the dam. Angle left off the bridge; just past the house's garden go right up the path, then driveway, to a lane. Turn right. At the 'No Entry' wooden gates continue along the driveway (public footpath), pass between the house and stables and remain with the track to reach the sailing club slipways. Cross the brook and turn right on the roadway past a barrier. Just past the parking area fork left between bollards. Passing above cottages, the path reaches a causeway bridge. Cross this.

2. For the short walk turn right and head back to the start. Otherwise, turn left on the track beside this upper arm of Jumbles Reservoir. The name Jumbles is derived from a local dialect word, 'Dumbles', meaning a watery ravine. The paved path forges up this wooded chasm to reach the first buildings at Turton Bottoms. Continue to the cross-way.

3. Turn left over the bridge and up the road. In 120 yards fork right onto a path and across a railed old packhorse bridge. Beyond the first cottages turn right along a cobbled lane, Birches Road. Swing right on the gravelly track at the end of the terrace and start a gentle climb out of Bradshaw Brook valley to hillside pastures.

4. In 500 yards, at Birches Farm, turn right through the farmyard. Beyond the cattle grid and parking, look left (towards a barn) for a low gap-stile into pasture and turn right on a path, with a stone wall on your right. From the stile at the next corner, advance across the heart of the field, cross a wooden footbridge (left of a tractor bridge) in the strip of trees, then head half-right, aiming well right of the farm soon visible ahead.

5. Look very carefully for the waymarked stile through the kinked fence above small ponds. Walk half-left off it down the wide earth track. In 40 yards turn left on a narrow grassy path just before the final pond. Climb the stile and advance to enter Walsh Fold farmyard (awkward gate).

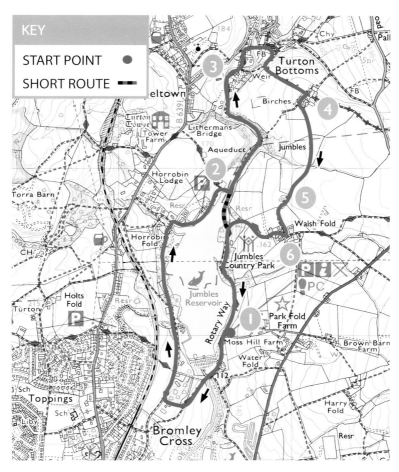

KEY

START POINT ●

SHORT ROUTE ▬▬

6. Immediately turn right, passing in front of the house to the single large tree just past the last barn and gate. Head three-quarters right here (not the field road), past the field-centre waymarked post to the lowest corner of the pasture, from where a path (Rotary Way) drops through the woods to the reservoir. Turn left to the start.

MERSEY VALLEY

STROLL BETWEEN TWO METROLINK STATIONS ALONG THE VERDANT VALLEY OF THE MERSEY IN THE FOOTSTEPS OF BONNIE PRINCE CHARLIE.

The leafy suburbs to the south of Manchester slope gently to the bank of the River Mersey as it meanders across the edge of the Cheshire Plain. A few farms nibble at the riverside meadows, but apart from a few areas of suburban sprawl and an industrial unit or two, the valley is largely undeveloped.

There's good reason for this. The river is prone to flooding and its vigorous character has seen its course move from side to side across the wide valley. Just downstream of this walk, a waterside pub has been recorded historically as being on the Lancashire bank some decades: Chesire in others! The migrating Mersey marks the traditional boundary between Lancashire and Cheshire. It's only actually called the Mersey from Stockport downstream, which is where the lively rivers Tame and Goyt meet.

This walk first heads for the low ridge of Heaton Mersey Common, from which extensive views sweep across southern Manchester towards the distant Mersey Estuary, the low hills in West Lancashire and the shapely West Pennine Moors. We then slide down through the conservation village to reach the northern bank of the Mersey at the site of a vast mill complex, long lost to history.

Heading downstream, we pass a string of spinneys and watery, reedy byes and flood basins (golf courses!) which now characterise the valley. The sturdy embankments are partly the result of flood management schemes and partly from the construction of the M63 motorway (now the M60) in the 1970s.

Over the past 30 years a huge clean-up campaign has seen the once heavily polluted waterway blossom into a linear park rich with wildlife and wildflowers. Salmon and otters have returned to the river, whilst kingfishers and goosander ducks point to the cleanliness of the waters here. Canoeists and anglers tackle the rapids and pools where chemical cocktails once brewed.

The transformation is extraordinary; and whilst the drone of the M60 and flights using

nearby Manchester Airport can prove a distraction, the pocket woods, wildflower meadows and popular Trans-Pennine Trail offer a pleasant escape from the hubbub of the nearby town and city centres. This is a walk brimming with potential surprises and discoveries, from the industrial heritage of Mersey Vale Nature Park to the tantalising willow carrs and botanical gardens below Didsbury's medieval church.

NOTE: For public transport, Metrolink trams to East Didsbury terminus; buses and trains to East Didsbury (Tel: Traveline 0871 200 2233)

THE BASICS

Distance: 5 miles / 8km

Gradient: Mostly level, with one short easy climb

Severity: Easy

Approximate time: 2½ to 3 hrs

Stiles: None

Map: OS Explorer 277 (Manchester and Salford)

Path description: Firm paths, tracks and lanes, muddy in places

Start point: East Didsbury Metrolink Station (GR: SJ 856905)

Parking: East Didsbury Metrolink Station (free) (M19 1TB)

Dog friendly: Not allowed in botanic gardens rockery or on Metrolink trams (except guide/hearing dogs)

Public toilets: Facilities in Didsbury

Nearest refreshment: Pubs along the way, all services in Didsbury Village

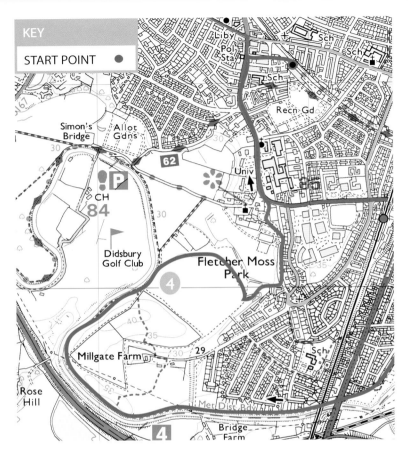

KEY

START POINT ●

Simon's Bridge
Allot Gdns
Recn Gd
62
Univ
!P
CH
84
Didsbury Golf Club
Fletcher Moss Park
4
Millgate Farm
29
Sch
Rose Hill
Mer Dist BdY
4
Bridge Farm

1. Use the underpass beyond the Metrolink terminus at East Didsbury. Stay ahead-left at the fork to reach the crossing of Meltham Road; turn left to the Griffin Inn. Slip right of the pub into Harwood Road; then past the driving range to the road end at barriers. Beyond these turn right on Berwick Avenue, then in 100 yards right into Rosgill Close. In 50 yards turn right through an area of garages to a gate onto Heaton Mersey Common. Go left, soon putting ponds on your right. Beyond these

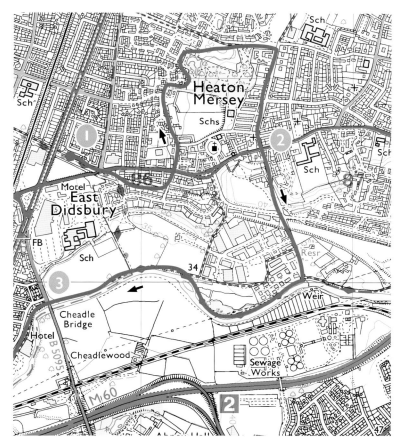

pass through the band of trees and then go half-right up the grassy slope. At the top take the path ahead along the left fringe of the Common below huge beech trees. At the gated entrance half-right beyond a sub-station turn right on Mersey Road and walk to its end.

2. Cross diagonally into Vale Close, beside the Crown Inn, and descend this cobbled way past terraced cottages. At the bottom, continue on the road beside the industrial units, and at the bend slip ahead to the

MERSEY VALLEY WALK

Mersey. An information board above the weir here details the industrial history of this area. Turn right and follow the path beside the river for nearly a mile (1.5km) to Cheadle Bridge.

3. Cross the road and walk to The Waterside Hotel. Beyond the far car park join the path past old tennis courts and into a copse of willow and alder. Pass beneath the main road and railway. It was hereabouts in 1745 that Bonnie Prince Charlie (Charles Edward Stuart, pretender to the throne) crossed the river at a ford, leading his ill-fated Jacobite Scots forces towards Derby. Stick with the riverside path for 1500 yards to reach a major junction of paths as the Mersey swings left, 750 yards after power cables cross the river.

4. Turn back-right to a bank-top crossing of tarred paths. Here turn left (not sharp left) onto the wide, hard-standing path into Stenner Woods (signed 'Health Walk'). The way curls within the fringe of the trees (meadow to your right) reaching a fork in 800 yards by metal gates. Turn left onto the right-hand path, following the boardwalk through the woods. At the end up steps turn left to Fletcher Moss Park. The gardens form the Manchester Botanical Gardens; spend time exploring the labyrinthine paths before joining the main road next to the Didsbury pub.

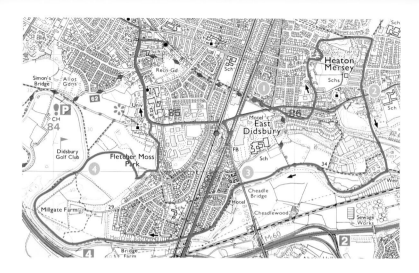

Bear left to the village centre, and find the Post Office (on Albert Hill Street opposite Boots) beyond which is the Fletcher Moss pub. Didsbury Village Metrolink station is behind this.

DIGGLE

FOLLOW THE PENNINE BRIDLEWAY TO DISCOVER BRITAIN'S LONGEST CANAL TUNNEL ON A WALK THROUGH OLD WEAVING HAMLETS IN THE STRIKING COUNTRYSIDE OF THE UPPER TAME VALLEY.

The Upper Tame Valley is a hilly area of hamlets of mellow stone houses, many dating from before the Industrial Revolution gathered pace around 250 years ago. The attractive gritstone buildings often have a distinctive range of mullioned windows across their upper storeys. These 'weaver's galleries' were designed to let in as much daylight as possible to allow workers to operate hand-looms, long before the days of the huge steam-driven mills that still dot the area. The walk starts near the Brownhill Countryside Centre at Uppermill. It's a superb setting beneath the towering viaduct and next to one of the deepest locks on the canal network.

The route rises gently to forge a way along the lower flank of Saddleworth's enfolding moors. You're on the Pennine Bridleway National Trail; here it's a tranquil track harvesting the wonderful panorama across deep vale and moody uplands that focus on Standedge Edge. This commanding moorland ridge marks the line of the Pennines and is England's great watershed – becks rising here head either east to the North Sea or west to the Irish Sea. In Diglea it's worth wandering up the village lane in front of the pub to appreciate the heritage architecture here.

On the longest option, the route circles the reedy moorland fringe and returns to Diglea along a rough lane emerging beside the pub. This, Boat Lane, was the route taken by barge horses across the moorland. They were unable to pull barges through the canal tunnel which passes beneath the hills here, as it had no towpath. The narrowboats were moved through the tunnel by professional 'leggers', who lay on their backs on the boat's cabin top and 'walked' along the roof of the tunnel, thus propelling the boat along.

The Huddersfield Narrow Canal was completed in 1811 with the opening of the Standedge Tunnel, the longest (3 miles, 135 yards/4950m), highest above sea level (645ft/196m) and deepest underground (636ft/194m) in Britain. The walk passes the southern portal of this tunnel at Diggle. It's only wide enough for one boat, so a one-way system is operated, and it takes around two hours to pass through. The canal became derelict in the 1920s and remained so for 70 years before a dedicated band of volunteers reopened this magnificent trans-Pennine waterway in 2001.

NOTE: For Public transport, Buses to Brownhill Countryside Centre from Oldham, Manchester and Ashton-under-Lyne (Tel: Traveline 0871 200 2233)

THE BASICS

Distance: (short) 2 miles / 3km (medium) 3 miles / 4.5km (long) 4½ miles / 7.2km

Gradient: Several modest slopes, otherwise largely level; steps over railway footbridge; two farm gates to use

Severity: Easy

Approximate time: 1½ to 3 hrs

Stiles: None

Map: OS Explorer OL1 (The Peak District – Dark Peak Area)

Path description: Tarred lanes, field paths, farm roads, canal towpath

Start point: Wool Road car park (free), Uppermill (GR: SD 995065)

Parking: Car park off the main A670 road, 200 yards past the mini-roundabout just above Brownhill Countryside Centre (OL3 5QR)

Dog friendly: On long leads

Public toilets: Brownhill Countryside Centre and The Diggle Hotel

Nearest refreshment: Diggle Hotel Diglea; Navigation Inn Uppermill; Canalside cafés

DIGGLE WALK

1. Walk beside the canal (right) to the nearby Brownhill Countryside Centre. Return to the car park and cross diagonally left over the main road onto the cobbles. Take the grass-centred track between house numbers 18 and 20. Keep ahead off the sharp bend and cross the railway footbridge. An enclosed path reaches a pasture; aim right of the farm outbuildings to join a lane and keep left at the adjacent junction.

2. At the next buildings in 450 yards, slip left along the cobbled entry (Pennine Bridleway). This becomes a sandy track, shortly reaching more buildings and a concreted lane. Keep right at the fork in 100 yards; then at the T-junction go left to a triangular junction. For the short walk head left 400 yards to cross the canal; turn left on the towpath past firs to return to the start. Otherwise; bear right through the dip and remain on the lane to reach the Diggle Hotel pub. The medium option heads left over the railway bridge.

3. The longest walk heads right along the lane in front of the pub. Presently; join the 'Private Road' – it is a public path. In another 400 yards turn left up the lane for Diggle House Farm. At the bend beyond the first house fork left up the walled track. At the top, keep left on the path above the wall to reach the houses at Diggle End. Immediately past these turn left on the descending track. Boat Lane is the old barge-horse route over the moors and winds back to the Diggle Hotel. Cross over the railway (where the medium walk rejoins) and bend left to the Sam Road car park.

4. Join the towpath at the rear of the car park. Here you'll see the southern portal of Standedge Tunnel. Follow the towpath down into the Tame Valley; at any lock before 25W, cross to the left bank. The towpath eventually passes beneath the main road in a concrete tunnel. On the right here is the Wool Road Transhipment Wharf, where goods were transferred from narrowboat to packhorse before the Standedge Tunnel opened. You're back!

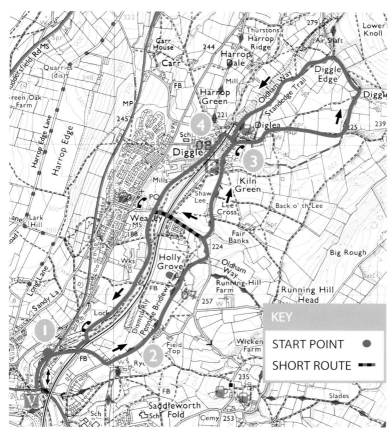

MELLOR MOOR

Minimum effort is needed to maximise the huge panoramic views on a moorland lane circuit where a famous author gained inspiration high above the Goyt Valley.

Mellor's parish church stands at a remote spot high above the village. This modest advantage in height reaps the reward of tremendous views along the rippling edges of the Peak District. Iron Age tribespeople constructed a hill fort here around 2,200 years ago, on a site that also has produced Bronze Age artefacts over 3,500 years old.

Excavations have revealed part of the long history of the defended site. Next to the churchyard a series of pits have been tidied up and made easy to view, with information boards. A nearby reconstruction of an Iron Age roundhouse hints at how those ancient inhabitants may have lived.

This walk begins from the church car park. It's worth exploring St Thomas' Church, whose font may date back to Viking times and whose 700-year-old pulpit is thought to be the oldest in England. The wide track and then field road roughly follows the line of the huge enclosure that once incorporated the hillfort. The panorama of Kinder Scout seems to improve with every step. The route meets with the tarred moorland lane, Shiloh Road and drifts on this usually quiet way to woodland at Broadhurst Edge and great views south towards the heart of the Peak.

A series of age-old walled moorland tracks is followed for the next mile and more. Between spring and midsummer the banks explode with colourful wildflowers; skylarks sing incessantly and buzzards quarter the skies silently overhead. In time the walk reaches a crossways and tarred lane. To the left here can be seen the roofline of a farmhouse called Three Chimneys, which may have been the model for the cottage where The Railway Children lived in the famous novel of that name. The author of the book, Edith Nesbit, stayed with relatives at a nearby house; the description of the railway, tunnel and viaduct in the book closely matches the views from here of the line in the valley below, now largely obscured by vegetation. The house is not open to visitors.

The route descends gradually, offering lovely views across the wooded trough of the Goyt Valley to the distant skyline of central Manchester. The walk presently reaches Mellor village and the Devonshire Arms pub. Time to rest and recuperate before a final flourish up the lane back to the hilltop church.

THE BASICS

Distance: 4 miles / 6.5km
Gradient: Undulating; short climb back to finish
Severity: Easy
Approximate time: 2½ hrs
Stiles: Two
Map: OS Explorer OL1 (The Peak District – Dark Peak Area)
Path description: Sandy tracks, tarred lanes, rough byways, field paths
Start point: Mellor Church (GR: SJ 983889)
Parking: Large free car par opposite church (SK6 5LX)
Dog friendly: On leads as necessary
Public toilets: Facilities for customers at Devonshire Arms
Nearest refreshment: Devonshire Arms pub, Mellor
Public transport: Bus 375 to the Devonshire Arms from Stockport (Tel: Traveline 0871 200 2233)

1. Join the level, tarred lane between the Old Vicarage and the car park. Where this turns left, keep ahead through the gate-side hand gate along the field-edge track. More hand gates advance the way past hilltop beech trees. Simply remain with this track, perhaps muddy in places. At the crossways signed for Hambleton Fold Farm, go ahead on the tarred lane for 50 yards; then turn left off the bend on the rough walled lane, reaching Shiloh Road in another 600 yards.

2. Turn right. The generally quiet road allows lovely views across to the curve of Lantern Pike and the heights of Kinder beyond. At the five-way junction keep ahead on the rougher walled track, Pole Lane (this forms the Greater Manchester and Derbyshire county boundary.) Follow it to Broadhurstedge Plantation oakwoods nature reserve, alive with wild birds, including springtime cuckoos.

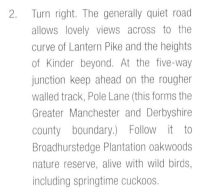

3. At the far edge of the plantation turn right on the tarred road, Primrose Lane; beyond Napkinpiece Farm curling gradually right to a junction in 450 yards. Turn left along the gradually rising Black Lane, another of the web of byways on Mellor Moor that are justly popular with horseriders and ramblers. Off to the left are the jumbled gritstone hills of north-east Cheshire; the sharp-eyed will pick out

The Cage folly in Lyme Park. Just after the crest, slip through the metal hand gate,

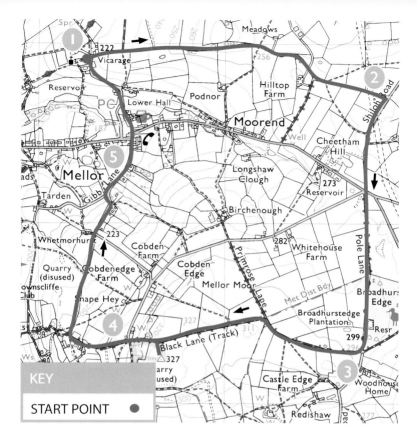

left, to divert to the nearby triangulation pillar on Cobden Edge, an extraordinary viewpoint. Return to Black Lane and go left down to the crossways below the large wooden cross. The house roofline visible to the left is Three Chimneys.

4. Keep ahead down the tarred lane beneath the wires. At the golf course, turn right on the way that is waymarked for Mellor Church. Stick with the path just within the boundary wall. Beside the copse fork right to cross a low stile, still keeping the wall on your right to reach a low stile into a lane by a white cottage. Head downhill to reach a T-junction with Gibb Lane. Bear right through to Mellor village and the Devonshire Arms.

5. To the right of the pub a rougher lane drops beside the converted chapel. Follow this past the cottages to a tarred lane and walk up this to return to Mellor Church.

GOYT VALLEY

Verdant woodlands clothe the site of one of England's largest mills on a canal and riverside ramble in the pretty Goyt Valley.

A great quiz question is: 'Where does the River Mersey rise?' A trick question, as the answer is, it doesn't. Rather, it is formed by the confluence of two rivers in the centre of Stockport. One of these is the River Goyt; this undulating ramble explores the middle reaches of this swiftly flowing watercourse, a fascinating area of woodlands, torrents and absorbing industrial heritage tucked into a deep valley on the fringe of the Peak District National Park.

A short climb from Marple Station finds the towpath of the Peak Forest Canal. A lock beside a converted warehouse marks the halfway point of a flight taking the canal down from the valley side towards the heart of Manchester. The canal was built to allow the movement of limestone from huge quarries in the Peak District hills to the heartland of Manchester, the industries here and the farmlands beyond where lime was used to make farming the clayey soils easier.

At the top of the locks the canal splits. The Macclesfield Canal, one of the last to be built, in 1831, heads right; this walk heads left along the Upper Peak Forest Canal, opened in 1804. It's a tranquil, level walk along a stretch strewn with wildflowers in spring and summer. Superb views open out towards the great domes of moorland and sharp upland valleys marking the forbidding mass of Kinder Scout, the heart of the Dark Peak. The route leaves the canal to drop into the Goyt Valley's deep, wooded gorge, rich with wild birds. Crossing a graceful packhorse bridge at Strawberry Hill, the walk soon reaches the site of Mellor Mill. Once the largest such complex in the country, the huge cotton yarn mill was developed by the Georgian industrialist Samuel Oldknow and opened in 1792. The tranquil millponds now known as Roman Lakes fed vast waterwheels that powered cotton-spinning looms worked by 550 people. Young apprentices were housed in dormitories built behind the imposing house, Bottoms Hall.

Mellor Mill remained one of England's largest and most spectacular industrial buildings until destroyed by fire in 1892. It was Oldknow who was a major financer of the Peak Forest Canal, which allowed him to export his spun cotton yarn and cloth by canal boat to Manchester and beyond. Tranquil byways thread back to nearby Marple Bridge.

NOTE: For Public transport, Marple Station is on the regular daily train service linking Manchester Piccadilly with New Mills Central (and Sheffield); frequent buses to Marple Bridge from Stockport (Tel: Traveline 0871 200 2233)

THE BASICS

Distance: 4 miles / 6.5km
Gradient: Two short gentle climbs, otherwise largely level
Severity: Easy
Approximate time: 2½ hrs
Stiles: None
Map: OS Explorer OL1 (The Peak District – Dark Peak Area)
Path description: Canal towpath, tarred roads, unsurfaced byways
Start point: Marple railway station (GR: SJ 965893)
Parking: Public car park 200 yards downhill from station on the right (free) (SK6 7DA)
Dog friendly: On leads as appropriate
Public toilets: None
Nearest refreshment: Pubs and cafés in Marple Bridge; tearoom at Roman Lakes

GOYT VALLEY WALK

1. Walk uphill from the car park or railway station to the canal. Turn left along the towpath, with the water to your left. Opposite is the sturdy old warehouse, with its transhipment wharves still visible. Beyond lock 12 the path passes through a horse-tunnel, allowing barge horses to negotiate a way past the lock immediately below Posset Bridge. The blanked-off bridge arch was the canal arm to huge lime-kilns that once stood here. Continue beside the canal; the large side-ponds on the far side store water needed to supply the flight of locks.

2. Lock 16 is the highest of the flight which raises the canal 210 feet (65m) from the Goyt Valley. Cross the bridge here at Marple Junction. Below, the Macclesfield Canal heads south towards the heart of Cheshire; our route remains with the Peak Forest and rejoins the towpath just past the bridge, with the canal on your left. Change sides at Bridge 19, a corkscrew 'roving' bridge (allowing horses to change banks without being unhitched) and proceed along the wildflower-rich section to reach Bridge 21.

3. Turn left here to descend Plucksbridge Road and cross directly over the main road into the wooded track. Drop past secluded houses to cross the eye-catching bridge across the River Goyt. This is known as Roman Bridge because of the way it was constructed; it's actually a packhorse bridge built perhaps 400 years ago. Turn left on the rough lane, soon passing Floodgates Cottage, from where the nearby weir was managed. The waters fed into huge mill lodges (ponds) which still exist as the popular 'Roman Lakes' beyond the railway viaduct. Past the lakes, keep left at the fork near Bottoms Hall.

4. At the far end of the next millpond stood Mellor Mill; 400 feet (122m) long, six storeys high and powered by three waterwheels. Turn right at the fork along Bottoms Mill Road; in the woodlands hereabouts archaeological digs are rediscovering some of the mill's secrets. Remain with the old lane up the gentle

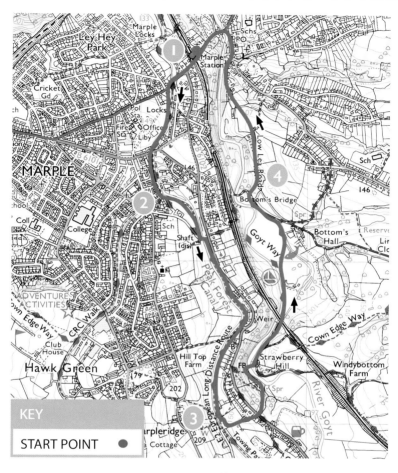

KEY

START POINT ●

hill before descending into Marple Bridge. Keep left to the bridge and traffic lights; here cross the Goyt to return to the car park and station.

CARRBROOK

A tantalising mix of industrial heritage, medieval history, World War II memories and gnarled old woodlands on this undulating walk along the flank of the Tame Valley.

The wild, high land on the eastern fringe of the Greater Manchester conurbation can often seem to be a bleak, featureless wilderness, an endless succession of moors, mosses, pikes and cloughs with an aura of inaccessibility and remoteness. Peel back the cover, however, and you'll find an intriguing area of woods, valleys and watercourses ripe for easy exploration. One such location that nibbles at the edges is at the village of Carrbrook.

The village is older than it looks, with a history going back to medieval times. It's the industrial heritage that immediately takes the eye, though. Old lodges (ponds) around the village recall long-gone small-scale woollen and cotton mills; whilst the huge Buckton Vale bleaching and calico printworks once plugged the mouth of Cowbury Dale and dominated the lives of the locals. The neat terraces of gritstone cottages were built between the 1870s and 1920s as a planned industrial village, with the employers providing everything from housing to recreational and leisure facilities.

The walk threads up Cowbury Dale past the site of parts of the mill to reach a reservoir. This was created in the 1890s to guarantee a supply of clean water for the bleaching processes. The walk in parts follows the tramroad used to transport materials to the site. Turning back, the route then heads through the delightful woodland fringing Buckton Castle Hill.

Buckton Castle was probably built for Ranulf, Earl of Chester in the 12th century, a stone fortress sited to control passage through the Tame Valley from the moors and the valuable hunting hereabouts. It was derelict by the 1350s and only rediscovered in 2008; there's little now to be seen at the site. The hill, however, played an important role in the Second World War when it was the site of a 'Starfish' decoy. These were built to fool the crews of Luftwaffe bombers into thinking they were over major targets so that they would drop their bombs on remote areas, rather than the real targets such as Manchester and Salford Docks. The decoys were laid out like streets and set ablaze at night to look like the target towns; Buckton Hill was one of 11 sites used to protect Manchester. Looping back past Micklehurst's high level Cricket Club, the walk returns to Carrbrook through the oldest parts of the village, dating back to the 1700s.

Take care on the two main road sections between points 3 and 5.

NOTE: For Public transport: Buses 343 & 344 from Oldham and Hyde and 348 from Ashton-under-Lyne run to Buckton Vale Institute, opposite the start (Tel: Traveline 0871 200 2233)

THE BASICS

Distance: 2¼ miles / 3.5km or 3¼ miles / 5.25km

Gradient: Several gradual ascents and descents; longer route has two climbs

Severity: Easy (moderate on longer route)

Approximate time: 1½ to 2½ hrs

Stiles: Three (short route) Five (long route)

Map: OS Explorer OL1 (The Peak District – Dark Peak Area)

Path description: Tarred lanes, rough tracks, woodland paths. Two main road sections

Start point: Buckton Vale Road, Carrbrook (GR: SD 988010)

Parking: Castle Clough car park (free), Carrbrook (SK15 3PG)

Dog friendly: No dogs in nature reserve (reservoir)

Public toilets: None

Nearest refreshment: Stamford Arms, Heyheads, Stalybridge or Mossley

CARRBROOK WALK

1. Join Long Row, upstream beside the beck, then slip left over the bridge into Cowbury Green park. From the far top corner turn right on the rough track. From the gate-side stile in 220 yards continue up the track for another 175 yards to a Nature Reserve board, then fork right to the reservoir in Cowbury Dale. Return down to the gate and turn right on the path into the woods; in a dozen paces step up to walk the higher path, going straight ahead past a redundant stile. It's a firm, undulating path through these extraordinary sessile oak woods. Nearing woodland-edge cottages, fork right (waymarked) on a much narrower path above the buildings to a corner stile into a long, sloping pasture. Head to the far-bottom corner stile.

2. For the shorter walk take the lane in front of Castle Farm to a track, left, by telephone masts in 250 yards (Point 4). For the longer walk, turn right 30 paces; then left up the rougher Moor Edge Road (Pennine Bridleway). This rises across the flank of Buckton Hill. In half-a-mile (1km) it bends sharply left over a brook; then rises to a fine junction immediately before power cables cross. Use the narrow gap-stile (no waymark) by the old gatepost on your left, aiming downfield to the left of the cottage, then down the very rough wall-side path to the main road. Beware traffic!

3. Turn left to the junction in 150 yards. Fork left up steep Castle Lane to Micklehurst Cricket Club. At the far end is a compound of masts, beyond which a rough grass-centred lane departs right.

4. Turn along this (the short walk rejoins here), snaking easily downhill to meet Huddersfield Road at a bend. Turn right along the verge for 50 paces to improve visibility; then cross to the pavement and head left along it, walking this main road pavement for 450 yards to reach a hillcrest crossways at Staley Road (The Stamford Arma is ahead on the right).

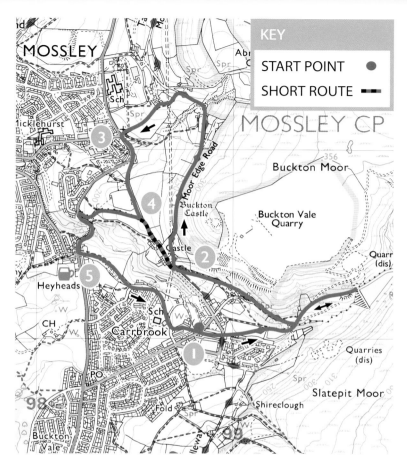

KEY

START POINT ●

SHORT ROUTE ▬▬

MOSSLEY

Micklehurst

MOSSLEY CP

Buckton Moor

Buckton Vale Quarry

Moor Edge Road

Buckton Castle

Castle

Heyheads

Quarry (dis)

CH

Carrbrook

Quarries (dis)

Fold

Shireclough

Slatepit Moor

Buckton Vale

5. Go left on the rough lane; this crests before dropping to a fork at a terrace. Go left, presently going through a gate across the lane. In another 200 yards go left at the fork, following this lane back to the car park.

CHADKIRK VALE

Explore the verdant woodlands, tranquil towpaths and peaceful pastures of the Etherow Valley, with a farm café and ancient chapel to discover along the way.

The wildfowl-rich lake at Compstall is a tantalising reminder of the many mills that once worked here beside the River Etherow. It was impounded about 1815 to help power large cotton-spinning and calico printing mills.

The walk follows the Etherow downstream through riverside woods before rising easily past the Watermeetings farms. The name reflects the meeting of the rivers Etherow and Goyt just off the walk route. Past a small housing estate the countryside soon reasserts its hold; beyond a railway the woodland towpath of the Peak Forest Canal is joined at the northern portal of Hyde Bank Tunnel before reaching the hamlet of Burymewick.

Below this is Chadkirk Estate, with its walled garden, wildflower meadows renowned for cowslips and the restored Tudor chapel of St Chad's. It's a tranquil spot nestled in Chadkirk Vale below Kirk Wood, one of the oldest in Greater Manchester. The walk turns back here, rising through the woods to the canal towpath and along to Marple Aqueduct.

The aqueduct striding across the deep valley of the River Goyt is one of the highlights of the British canal network, towering 100 feet (30m) above the river. Pierced with roundels to lessen its overall weight, it commands the gorge alongside its later twin, the railway viaduct of 1862.

The canal itself is one end of an astonishing feat of engineering built to allow the movement of limestone from the highland Peak District quarries to the markets of the lowlands. A system of horse-drawn and counterbalanced tramroads, the Peak Forest Tramway, snaked across the moors near Buxton, moving limestone down inclined planes to a complex of wharves and canal basins at Bugsworth, near Whaley Bridge some six miles (10km) from Marple. Here the limestone was crushed and loaded into canal barges, or burned first to produce lime and then loaded for onward

transport. The tramroad opened in 1796, at the same time as parts of the canal, and closed in 1925. The canal became disused in the 1950s, but was reopened as a leisure waterway in 1974.

A path slips down from the towpath halfway up the flight of locks to enter the mature woodlands of Brabyns Park. The track across the recreational parkland crosses a fine cast-iron bridge, dating from 1813 and one of the earliest and last-surviving such Georgian iron structures.

NOTE: For Public transport, Buses 383/4 to Compstall from Stockport (Tel: Traveline 0871 200 2233)

THE BASICS

Distance: 5 miles / 8km

Gradient: Several short ascents and descents, some steps in woodland

Severity: Easy

Approximate time: 3 hrs

Stiles: Two or three

Map: OS Explorer 277 (Manchester and Salford)

Path description: Unsurfaced riverside and woodland paths, farm lanes, canal towpath, tarred roadways

Start point: Etherow Country Park, Compstall (GR: SJ 966909)

Parking: Pay-and-display car park at Etherow Country Park (SK6 5JD)

Dog friendly: On leads

Public toilets: At start

Nearest refreshment: Cafés at start and at Hydebank Farm

CHADKIRK VALE WALK

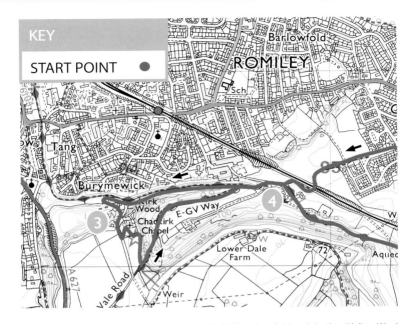

KEY

START POINT ●

1. Return to the main road and turn left. At the river bridge join the 'Valley Way' downstream beside the River Etherow through Redbrow Wood. At a fork keep left above the river; the path soon crosses pasture to reach Lower Watermeetings Farm. Beyond the farmyard the lane rises to Cherry Tree estate. Keep ahead.

2. At the T-junction in 150 yards turn left, then first right into Cherry Tree Lane, then left on Gotherage Lane. Go ahead on the path beside the play area, advancing over a railway bridge before reaching the complex at Hydebank Farm. Keep the buildings on your left. Just beyond them, fork left down the concrete track, under a bridge onto the towpath of the Peak Forest Canal.

3. In 600 yards are a white cottage and terrace of cottages down to your left. Descend the steps off the towpath here and turn left to Chadkirk, and in 350 yards go left into the grounds of Chadkirk Chapel (open weekend afternoons). Put

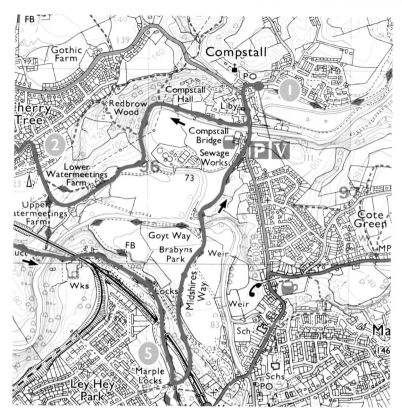

the walled garden on your left and walk round two sides to a woodland-foot path. Turn right; in 150 yards turn left up widely spaced steps for Peak Forest Canal. The path levels through these beechwoods, presently reaching the towpath once more. Turn right and walk back to Hydebank Farm. (Café here).

4. Keep right on Hyde Bank, a rough lane past Oakwood House; where the gates block the track, fork right to regain the canal at the southern end of the tunnel. Remain with the towpath; in half-a-mile (1km) crossing the aqueduct high above

the River Goyt. Beyond the railway overbridge keep left onto the towpath up beside the first six locks of the Marple Flight.

5. At lock 7 slip left on the path beside the wall, down steps and then fully left on the wide woodland track. This falls gradually, over first a railway then a wide cross-track with wooden railings, to a junction of ways just short of a brick building. Take the track past the barrier and to the right of the building. This wide way strikes across Brabyns Park to cross the River Goyt on a graceful cast-iron bridge. Stick with the track beyond to meet the main road. Turn left and cross the bridge to return to the nearby car park.

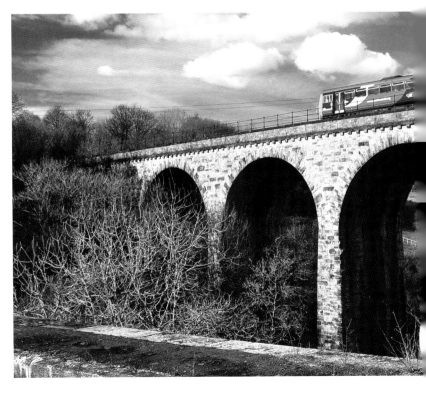

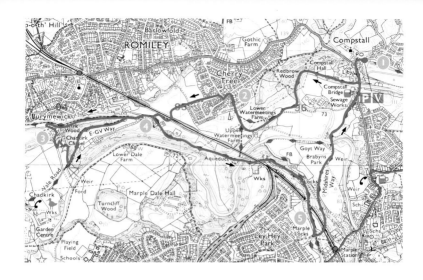

CHEW VALLEY

Gaze into an extraordinary chasm of a valley on this easy ramble around a reservoir and through cool woodland below Saddleworth Moor.

The high plateau of the Saddleworth Moors has been rent asunder, Chew Brook forming a marvellous, curving gorge in the landscape. A little to the north, the equally vigorous Greenfield Brook has carved out a similarly deep and eye-catching vale into the western flank of Black Hill. This pincer-like assault on the uplands comes together just to the east of the old mill town of Greenfield, where the two becks meet and mingle below the shapely snouts of two distinctive hills.

This refreshing walk investigates the two valleys, which today are partly drowned by the waters of Dovestone Reservoir. The dale below retains a string of mills which stretch to the River Tame further downstream. The reservoir is fringed by geometric plantations of fir trees, whilst stands of much older native oaks and beech stipple the steepening slopes to the south of the water.

Starting from the car park beside the dam the walk first joins a byway, Bradbury's Lane, cutting across the flank of Alphin Pike. This old walled track is part of a web of similar ways which have developed over the past 2,000 years; routes across the moors which avoid the once boggy and forested lowlands. Turning back from the secluded farm at Fern Lee the walk picks up the route of an old tramroad, laid to transport clay for lining Chew Reservoir in the early 1900s. At the time it was the highest reservoir in England.

Alphin Pike guards the southern side of the Chew Valley; to the north the shapely top of Alderman's Brow does the same job. The hills are named after two mythical giants, who both fell in love with the water-nymph Rimmon who lived in the river Chew. Rivals in love, they hurled great boulders at each other from the respective hilltops, creating the spectacular boulder-fields that this walk skims.

The tramroad passes through firwoods and then a lovely, wildlife-rich area of oakwoods before entering the mouth of Chew Valley. The walk follows it to meet the more recent reservoir service road just beyond an old bridge. Keen walkers can walk uphill along this to appreciate the scale of the gorge; our walk turns downhill to find a wide, sandy track that circles Dovestone Reservoir, cutting below gritstone cliffs and crossing the dam of the higher Yeoman Hay Reservoir before returning to the start through cool woodland.

THE BASICS

Distance: 5 miles / 8km

Gradient: A gentle, gradual climb to start, otherwise easily undulating

Severity: Easy

Approximate time: 3 hrs

Stiles: Two low stiles

Map: OS Explorer OL1 (The Peak District – Dark Peak Area)

Path description: Lanes and tracks, sandy paths; rough underfoot in places

Start point: Dovestone Reservoir (GR: SE 014035)

Parking: Reservoir car park, Bank Lane, Greenfield (pay & display) (OL3 7NE)

Dog friendly: On leads during lambing season (Feb-April)

Public toilets: At start

Nearest refreshment: The Clarence pub, Greenfield; Dovestone car park

Public transport: Buses run to The Clarence pub from Oldham & Manchester (180) and Oldham & Ashton-under-Lyne (350) (Tel: Traveline 0871 200 2233)

CHEW VALLEY WALK

1. From the upper end of the car park take the tarred Bradbury's Lane just above the toilet block. Beyond a long terrace of houses the road becomes a walled green lane, rising gradually above the mills in the valley below. It curls round to reach the houses at Fern Lee Farm.

2. Turn sharply back-left here on the path leading into a narrow, rough track. This rises gently between collapsed walls, presently skirting the top edge of a plantation of firs before plunging into the woods. The far side is reached soon enough, advancing across the lowest level of the eastern flank of Alphin Pike and merging with the line of the old tramroad. It's a good spot for a bit of upland birdwatching, with moorland species like wheatears, red grouse and ouzels perhaps revealing themselves. Beyond a couple of rough pastures and a hut, the woodland reappears as lovely upland oak and beech at Chew Piece, from which point there are excellent views across the valley to Dovestone Reservoir and the sharp cliffs marking the edge of Saddleworth Moor. Alderman's Brow is the round-snouted hill beyond the water. The trackbed of the meandering tramway eventually reaches a footbridge and a very short climb to the reservoir road.

3. The route is downhill, although a brisk, steeper detour uphill will reveal the astonishing valley more comprehensively. At the bottom, turn right at the junction just before the bridge over Chew Brook (path signed for Ashway Gap) and walk the path above Dovestone Reservoir (on your left), to reach and cross the dam of Yeoman Hey Reservoir.

4. At the far end, cross the spillway and turn left up the tarred lane. In 50 yards turn left onto the waymarked, gated track just before the woods. This charts a course above the waterline, with glorious views across to the sharp edges of Great and Little Dovestone Rocks, a favourite haunt of climbers. Upon reaching the near end of the dam, marked by a huge stepped overspill, walk the path over the footbridge and then along the top of the dam back to the start.

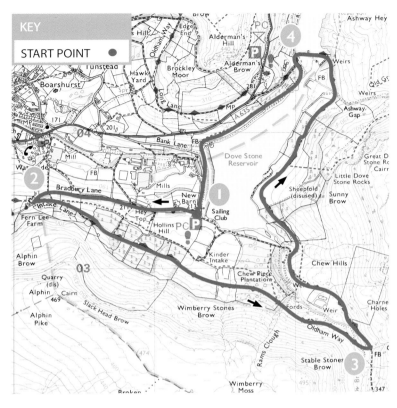

KEY

START POINT ●

SMITHILLS & BARROW BRIDGE

An undulating walk past some of Bolton's oldest buildings through countryside rippling across and between wooded cloughs at the edge of the Pennine moors.

We start from Moss Bank Park, a pleasant fringe-of-town municipal green park with oodles of extras, including a miniature railway and 'The Hive' Lancashire Wildlife Trust Centre. Staring near the vast brick chimney, remnant of an old mill at the far edge of the Park, the route then cuts through woodland and housing to reach the sublime Smithills Hall Country Park.

The magnificent half-timbered mansion at the core of the wooded domain has elements of medieval, Elizabethan and Victorian architecture, plus fine period furnishings and a very involved history. Much renovation was undertaken by the wealthy Ainsworths, who made a fortune from cloth bleaching in Victorian times. The route slips past the Hall into a wooded dingle, or dean, then rises to the estate open farm, a wonderful location for children to visit. There are entrance fees for both Hall and Farm, but not the parkland itself. In all the estate covers over 2,000 acres of woodland, dean, pasture and moorland threaded with popular paths.

Leaving the farm complex, good paths rise beside the Victorian estate's walled gardens to a higher track by one of the old estate farms. This modest gain in height opens out great views across Bolton's fringing countryside. The way then meanders on tracks and paths to reach the charming settlement of Barrow Bridge across a narrow stone bridge over fast-flowing Dean Brook.

This elongated little village was built as a 'model' industrial settlement by early Victorian entrepreneurs to house workers in the huge Dean Mills here. The smart villas we pass in this tranquil vale were home to the managers of the complex. Downstream of the bridge was a boating lake created in the old mill lodge; this closed in the 1950s. The millworkers' houses are below this again; nowadays peaceful terraces where once the noise of mill

machinery and steam engines rent the air. The settlement was visited by Prince Albert in 1851, whilst the Prime Minister and novelist Benjamin Disraeli featured the place as 'Milltown' in his 1844 novel Coningsby.

The shorter walk returns to the car park; the longer walk rises gently to cross the Old Links Golf Course – the first in Bolton, opened in 1891 – with great views of the West Pennine Moors from good field paths, returning down a redoubtable flight of 63 steps.

THE BASICS

Distance: 3 miles / 5km or 4½ miles / 7.25km
Gradient: A few gentle climbs; short moderate climb on longer route
Severity: Easy (moderate longer route)
Approximate time: 2 to 3 hrs
Stiles: Three
Map: OS Explorer 287 (West Pennine Moors)
Path description: Park tracks, farm lanes, woodland paths, tarred roads; muddy
Start point: Moss Bank Park, Bolton (GR: SD 694114)
Parking: Moss Bank Park main attractions car park, Barrow Bridge Lane, Bolton (BL1 6NQ) [NB: Not Moss Lane car park]
Dog friendly: On leads
Public toilets: Moss Bank Park
Nearest refreshment: Refreshments at Moss Bank Park; pubs in Halliwell
Public transport: Buses 501, 519 and 526 pass close to Moss Bank Park from Bolton bus station; services 525–7 serve Smithills (Tel: Traveline 0871 200 2233)

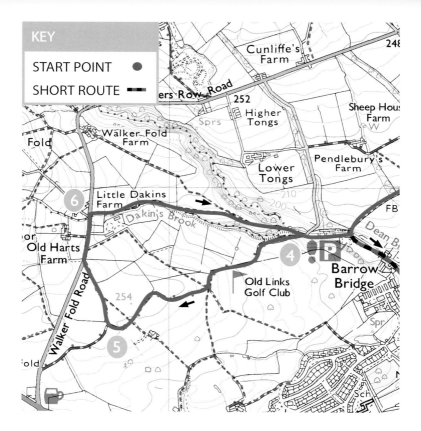

1. Turn right from the car park entrance. Turn left down Smithills Croft Road. At the sharp right bend slip left up the cobbled path rising through woodland; then go ahead on the fenced path between back gardens. Cross the estate road into another narrow path to a tarred road. Go ahead into Smithills Hall Park. At the junction bear right to reach Smithills Hall.

2. Keep right at the gates on a decent path which loops left past lawns fronting the Hall. Go up steps at the far end; turn left to pass the narrow end of the chapel. Turn right on the tree-edge path; in 50 yards slip left at railings onto a path into the dell. Cross the flat bridges and walk ahead-left up through the woods to a tarred lane; turn

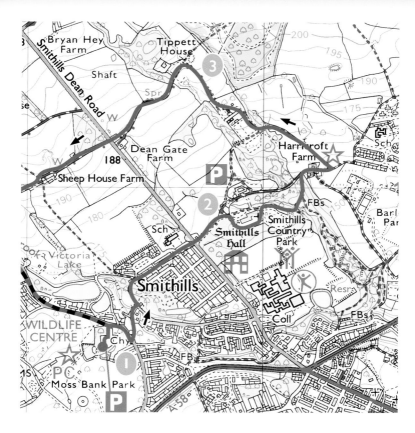

right to Smithills Open Farm. Keep ahead along the left-hand edge of the car park. At the far side turn left by a pylon on the fingerposted track up to a modern barn. Well-marked gates take the way across the access track and then up alongside a paddock. The path presently bends left into woodland. Beyond the redundant kissing gate, turn right up the wall-side path. Leave the woods on a wide track, rising to Tippett House.

3. Turn left on the improving lane to reach the main road by a derelict house. Look right for the continuing track to Sheep House Farm. Slip into the in-field path to pass immediately right of the farmhouse, then keep ahead fence-side

below cables. The path becomes an enclosed way and drops to a bridge over Dean Brook. Turn right into the upper part of Barrow Bridge (or turn left down the lane to return early to Moss Bank Park in 850 yards).

4. At the sharp bend fork ahead-left up the rising woodland path (signed Walker Fold Road), which levels as a sandy path across a golf course. Bend right with the path above tee 13 and remain with this widening track to and along the edge of the course.

5. Some 200 yards after it becomes cobbled; turn right onto the signed footpath at a corner. Advance across reedy pasture, then alongside the bushes. Keep left at the fork before turning right beside a broken wall (waymarked) on a path in line with the distant transmitter mast to a road. Turn right and walk the 220 yards to Edge Lane on your left.

6. Look right for the Barrow Bridge path by the shamrock-shaped boundary marker. This fenced path, occasionally awkward underfoot, runs above Dakin's Brook. Turn right off a stile, eventually merging with a wider path from the left. Keep ahead along the low ridge, soon descending the Miners' Steps then alongside Dean Brook to reach a lane. Go straight on, through Barrow Bridge to find the car park in 1,100 yards.

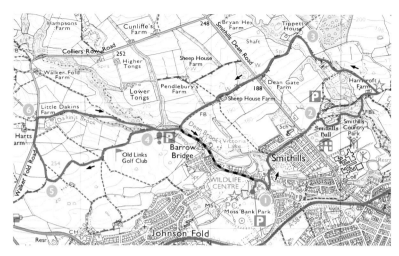

HOLLINGWORTH LAKE

Circle a placid lake in the shadow of the Pennines' lofty moors where Victorian day-trippers played at an inland resort.

On still days this great expanse of water reflects the enfolding hills and moors, snuggled as it is into the point where the South Pennines meet the West Pennines near Littleborough. It lies at the heart of a country park dappled with woodland and flower-rich pastures. In Victorian times it was popular with workers escaping the rigours of their jobs in the local mills; hence its nickname the 'Weighvers' Seaport'. Easy access by train from Rochdale and mill-towns in the West Riding of Yorkshire meant that it was their equivalent to a seaside trip. With a leisure park and amusements, boat trips and a beach, this was the consummate inland resort and remains a very popular place to visit.

It isn't a natural lake but, rather, a reservoir created to top up the nearby Rochdale Canal. First flooded in 1804, it supplements a line of reservoirs high in the hills to the east, to the north of the distinctive, bristly ridge of Blackstone Edge, which draws the eye to the Yorkshire horizon. The canal itself links central Manchester with Sowerby Bridge (near Halifax) via Rochdale, and was reopened in 2002 after falling into disuse in the 1930s.

There's a choice of two rambles here. Both start from the Visitor Centre at the Ealees car park and cross the dam before the shorter option diverges, continuing around the shoreline to complete an easy, level circuit of the water.

Along the way are wildflower and haymeadows and a birdwatching hide set on a low headland. The very appealing longer route slides away from the busy lakeside to rise gently along a farm lane towards the higher hills and moors. We don't reach any great height, nor is the climb at all steep; minimal effort unveils some tremendous views back across the lake to the West Pennines, a wide sweep across remote moorland to Knowl Hill's wind turbines and distant Winter Hill. It also crosses over the M62 motorway, highest in England, then finds the remarkably tranquil hidden valley of Longden Clough and the abandoned buildings of a water-powered textile mill. Nearby Rakewood village is peaceful now, but once had two woollen flannel mills, a few melancholic ruins of which remain. The longer ramble then joins the shorter on a clockwise circuit of the lake to return to the start.

NOTE: For Public transport, Regular daily buses 452, 455 & 456 to Hollingworth Lake from Rochdale and Littleborough (Tel: Traveline 0871 200 2233)

THE BASICS

Distance: 2½ miles / 4km or 4½ miles / 7.25km
Gradient: Short walk level; longer walk has a steady, gentle climb
Severity: Easy
Approximate time: 1½ or 3 hrs
Stiles: None
Map: OS Explorer OL21 (South Pennines)
Path description: Tarred lanes, firm lakeside paths; longer walk includes dirt tracks
Start point: Hollingworth Lake Visitor Centre (GR: SD 940152)
Parking: Hollingworth Lake Visitor Centre (pay & display) (OL15 0AQ)
Dog friendly: On long leads
Public toilets: At start
Nearest refreshment: Café at start; pubs, cafés restaurants at lakeside

HOLLINGWORTH LAKE WALK

1. From the Visitor Centre approach road turn left across Rakewood dam. At the dam's end is a fork in the road. The shorter walk remains on the level, wider road for another 450 yards to reach a stone 'island' in the road. Turn right here at the Country Park board and pick up the directions at Point 5. The longer route heads left up the part-cobbled lane in front of the cottages, signed 'Pennine Bridleway: Summit 4¼'.

2. The lane rises easily into the low hills edging Syke Moor. Passing by a few secluded houses, the old worn-flagged track drops to end at remote Syke Farm. Now join the rough gated track beyond, still the Pennine Bridleway. It's a gradual climb, with marvellous views behind. At a junction, keep right as the waymarked Pennine Bridleway forks left. Our route continues just outside the woods, presently reaching a walled corner and gate.

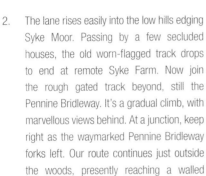

3. Don't use this gate; instead turn left and rise with the narrower path that keeps some way above the wall to your right. This way rises easily to reach a T-junction directly beneath the power lines. Turn right on the moorland road and pass through a gate to reach a house perched above the noisy M62 motorway.

4. Join the driveway and cross the motorway bridge. Turn right to the nearby farm and keep left, dropping steadily down the rough lane into the deep Longden End Clough. At the bottom are the striking buildings of Booth Hollings Mill, built in the 18th century and used as a fulling and bleaching mill processing wool and cotton until last century. Turn right; the rough lane shortly passes beneath Rakewood Viaduct, one of the most renowned structures on the M62. Beyond a cattle grid the lane becomes tarred. Remain with it down past houses and the skeletal stone

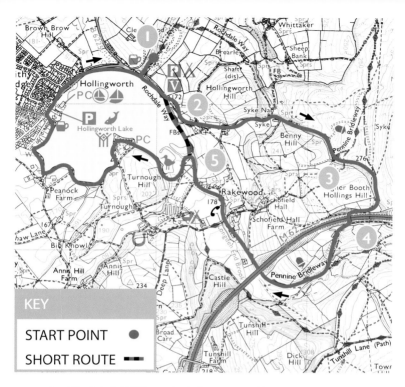

walls of the Schofield Mill complex before passing the entrance to Hollingworth Lake Caravan Park. Just past the small pond on your right you'll reach the entrance, left, to the country park.

5. Turn into here (short route rejoins) along the tarred lane which, passing above a bird hide, curls around to a lakeside café. Simply follow the lakeshore track all the way round to emerge beside The Beach pub-restaurant. Here turn right to walk the shoreline promenade to the junction in front of The Wine Press pub. Bear right to return to the car park.

DAISY NOOK & PARK BRIDGE

Woodlands, hidden heritage and glorious gorges nestle in the hidden valley of the River Medlock.

It's easy to miss the River Medlock on its short journey from the fringe of the Peak District's northern moors to Manchester city centre, where it meets with the River Irwell at Castlefield. This modest valley was the heartland of Manchester's industrial might; a jigsaw of iron and steel, heavy manufacturing, mining and mills that lit up the night skies for nearly 200 years.

The improvement of the valley is still an ongoing project, and the meandering valley is clawing its way back to greenness. One section has a head start in this. Marking the boundary between Oldham and Ashton, its wooded course offers easy access to some alluring countryside where the Pennines meet the Lancashire Plain. Old canals, tramroads and railways thread the valley, and a string of intriguing industrial heritage locations lie secluded amidst thick woodland and along winding gorges carved into the gritstone flanks of the Pennines.

We start from Daisy Nook, a country park based around a derelict canal interchange at Waterhouses. The flowery renaming was popularised by the famous Lancashire dialect writer Ben Brierley in Victorian times. The route diverts to reveal Crime Lake, a popular Edwardian day-trip destination which featured in a painting by L.S. Lowry. A secluded section of derelict canal is joined along the valley side, becoming a lovely wooded walk which eventually reaches the hidden hamlet of Park Bridge, tucked away in the deepest part of the Medlock's twisting valley.

The bridge where the walk leaves the woods to join a lane, Fenny Fields Bridge, is close to where one of the first-ever steam engines used to drain coalmines was sited. Built about 1760, 'Fairbottom Bob' worked until the 1830s when it was abandoned. Somehow it survived intact until the 1920s when Henry Ford (of the motor company) bought it and transported it to his private museum in the USA.

Park Bridge's ironworks eventually closed in 1963, after producing iron that was said to have been used as rivets in both the Eiffel Tower and the Titanic! Our stroll now rises past old housing connected with the works before squeezing into Rocher Vale, an impressive little gorge where mines, tramways and ironworks have left a fascinating footprint. The former Oldham, Ashton and Guide Bridge railway trackbed is followed before side paths string above a series of wooded cloughs to return to the start at Daisy Nook.

NOTE: For Public transport: Buses 168, 169 (Ashton to Chorlton) and 231 (Ashton to Manchester Piccadilly Gardens) run along Newmarket Road close to Daisy Nook. (Tel: Traveline 0871 200 2233)

THE BASICS

Distance: 5 miles / 8km
Gradient: Some gentle climbs and descents; a few easy steps
Severity: Moderate
Approximate time: 3 hrs
Stiles: Only gap-stiles
Map: OS Explorer: 277 (Manchester and Salford)
Path description: Towpath, woodland paths, lanes, firm tracks; some steps
Start point: Daisy Nook Country Park Visitor Centre (GR: SD 920005)
Parking: Daisy Nook (free) (M35 9WJ)
Dog friendly: On leads where appropriate
Public toilets: At start
Nearest refreshment: Cafés at start and at Park Bridge (closed Monday - Tuesday)

1.   Walk past the play area and pond. This is part of the old Hollinwood Canal which, beyond the cutting, crosses Waterhouses aqueduct high above the Medlock. Rise beside the former lock staircase; then turn left along the towpath, passing Sammy's Basin fishing pond, then over a spillway to reach Crime Lake (500 yards). Return to Sammy's Basin and bear left around it, joining the overgrown Fairbottom Branch Canal. Trace this secluded waterway to and through the underpass in half-a-mile (1km).

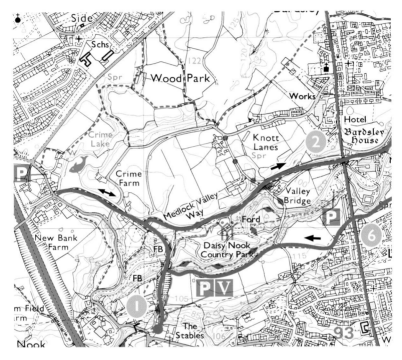

2.   Beyond a mill complex the woodland way continues between the old canal and the shaded gorge of the Medlock to your right. You'll reach Fenny Fields Bridge, where the canal met a tramroad which transported iron from the complex at Park Bridge. Bear right over the bridge, and then keep left at the junction to reach Park Bridge itself. Interpretive boards along the way detail what you're looking at and suggest short diversions. There's a heritage centre (limited opening) at the old stables.

3.   Uphill from the stables turn right before Dingle Terrace, in 400 yards reaching a T-junction beyond houses. Turn down the lane; at the barrier (left) near the hill-foot turn through the old car park, and then climb the grassy slope steps to find a footbridge over the Medlock. This peaceful, secluded clough of Rocher Vale was once bustling with mines and forges. Allow time to explore – carefully!

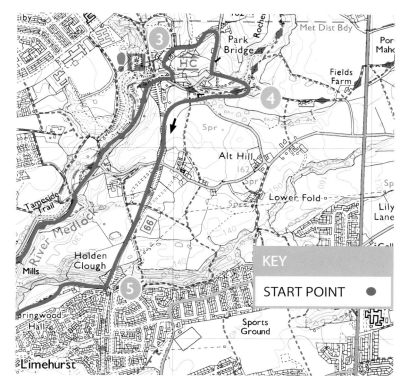

4. Head right off the footbridge; at the nearby 'Park Bridge' sign favour the inclined sandy track, the course of a former railway. Straight over the rough Alt Hill Road, the tarred track advances along the bed of the old Oldham to Guide Bridge line. Cross a tarred lane and continue ahead.

5. In another 900 yards, as housing appears, be alert for a huge pylon on the right. The waymarked path heads through a handgate here onto a compacted track by wooden fencing. Continue past Limehurst Farm and along the access lane to the main road.

6. Cross diagonally-right into Highfield Terrace and walk this for 220 yards to join a narrow, fenced field-path to the right across paddocks. Cross straight over the rough lane onto the continuing path beside a fence fringing Boodle Wood, and at the far end turn left along the old canal cutting back to Daisy Nook.

REDISHER WOOD

AN AIRY STROLL ALONG OLD MOORLAND LANES WHERE A
DRAMATIC MONUMENT DEDICATED TO A FORMER PRIME
MINISTER TOWERS ABOVE A WOODED VALE RICH WITH
WILDLIFE AND WATERFALLS.

High above Ramsbottom is Harcles (or Holcombe) Hill. Near the summit is the Peel Tower, dedicated to the Victorian Prime Minister and local MP Sir Robert Peel. It's a steep hike up to the top, so that's for the ambitious rambler. This walk instead curls around the snout of Holcombe Hill, revelling in the fine views and discovering a hidden heritage deep in the secluded, wooded valley of Holcombe Brook.

The hill itself is a popular local outing, with family groups making the climb from the steam railway station in Ramsbottom. The steep, final pitch is the location most years for a pace egg race on Good Friday, when painted, hard-boiled eggs are rolled down a course by children of all ages, egged on by garishly attired supporters who also perform a mumming play in the area's pubs. One of these is on the route of the walk; an ideal stop whether or not you're here on Good Friday!

The initial stage of the walk joins an old cobbled lane. To your right you'll see the spire of Holcombe's parish church. In 1916 this was damaged by bombs dropped from a Zeppelin; one of the first air raids in history. Turning along tranquil Moorbottom Road, the gently undulating walk passes above the eye-catching Darul Uloom Islamic College. Built as a private house in 1846 it was later used as a sanatorium.

Further along, the middle distance reveals the shooting ranges tucked into the deep cleft of the Red Brook. Before reaching the ranges, the walk drops down past ruined farms into the valley of the Holcombe Brook.

Below Saplin Wood a rake of old millponds are now drained and half-hidden in the trees. It's a curious mixture of industrial remains and ancient woodland. There were bleachworks, mills, small coal workings and quarries here. At the same time, Redisher Wood is amongst the oldest in the north-west; the steeper slopes have never been deforested whilst the presence of bluebells indicates centuries without major disturbance.

The valley is protected as a nature reserve and has a wealth of birds, from linnets and green woodpeckers to dippers and kingfishers, and a small herd of roe deer. Colourful heathland above the woods contrasts with the reedy old lodges where marsh marigolds and bulrushes take the eye. This really is a walk for all seasons.

NOTE: For Public transport, many buses to the Hare & Hounds from Bolton, Bury and Ramsbottom (Tel: Traveline 0871 200 2233)

THE BASICS

Distance: 3 miles / 5km
Gradient: A steady rise to finish, with a few short climbs and descents
Severity: Moderate
Approximate time: 2 to 2½ hrs
Stiles: Three gate-stiles
Map: OS Explorer 287 (West Pennine Moors)
Path description: Tarred and cobbled lanes, rough tracks, woodland paths, muddy in places
Start point: Holcombe (GR: SD 782163)
Parking: Peel Tower car park, Lumb Carr Road (B6214), towards Holcombe (BL8 4LZ)
Dog friendly: On leads
Public toilets: For customers only, at Hare & Hounds
Nearest refreshment: Hare & Hounds Inn, Holcombe Brook

REDISHER WOOD WALK

1. Cross from the car park entrance into the enclosed path opposite-left. At the top turn right up cobbled Holcombe Old Road. In 120 yards turn sharply left on Moorbottom Road. This rougher lane soon levels to contour the hillside, passing houses. In half-a-mile (1km) the track threads past Bank Top Farm, then through a gate across cobbles below a lone tree. In a further 300 yards are the scant ruins of Taylor's Farm on your left.

2. Immediately before the ruins, take the fingerposted gate/stile on the left (army notice here) into the sloping field, pass the fence-end and drop with the clear path to a handgate into the woods at the field-foot. Wind down the wooded path, emerging into lower pasture via a handgate. Look ahead-left for another ruin and head past a reedy pond up to this.

3. Here, keep ahead-left at the fingerpost (not right), tracing a route along the left flank of the low ridge, with a stream soon down to your left, heading directly for distant Manchester city centre.

4. About 50 yards beyond the next gate turn right (fingerpost), continuing past a bench and down a part-paved path into Redisher Wood. Bear left on the main path within the woods, undulating to a point just before a low old stone bridge over Red (Holcombe) Brook. A short diversion left finds pretty waterfalls in a leafy gully.

5. Cross the bridge (not the flat wooden bridge); then in 50 yards turn left to cross the larger, railed wooden bridge. Turn right alongside the former Redisher Lodge pond to reach the old dam. Drift left away from the beck alongside the old goit (mill feed); the way presently passes above the old Redisher Works factory, continuing then ahead on the tarred access lane. At the former factory gates, the way is left

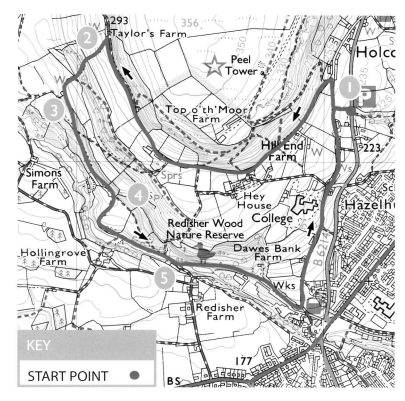

KEY

START POINT ●

up cobbled Holcombe Old Road (the Hare & Hounds is 75 yards ahead here). It's a constant, if gentle climb across the lowest slopes of Holcombe Hill. Cross straight over a tarred cross-lane, continuing ahead past cottages to find the path back to the car park on the right just past a final terrace of cottages.

PHILIPS PARK & PRESTWICH CLOUGH

Explore ancient woodland, the ghosts of industry and old parkland in the lower Irwell Valley just four miles from Manchester city centre, easily reached by Metrolink tram.

Between Bolton and Manchester a series of wooded cloughs nibbles deeply into the flank of a ridge of gritstone stretching from the distant high moors. A Roman Road was built along the ridge top; much later, settlements like Prestwich grew up along this routeway. The cloughs themselves, cut by tributaries of the River Irwell, became the location for industrial activity. This pleasant walk from ridge to river and back again discovers aspects of this heritage.

Mere Clough is a wooded vale bounding the southern edge of Philips Park. At the Irwell end were bleaching and dyeing works, powered by water from the Irwell and the little Bradley Brook. These textile complexes were founded by the Philips family, who built a substantial mansion at the edge of the woods, laying out walks and paths for their enjoyment. This walk, starting from the Metrolink Station at Prestwich, meanders down across Bradley Brook before slipping through Mid Wood, centuries-old woodland dotted with splendid oaks and birches. The woods formed part of a Norman deer park; occasionally roe deer are

seen these days, and there are blankets of woodland flowers in spring. The walk passes the remaining buildings of The Park mansion; the house was demolished in 1950 but the outbuildings survive at the heart of the parkland.

Kingfisher Lodge was the millpond for the Outwood Bleach Works; today it's home to many species of dragonflies and damselflies and noted for toads! The path reaches the Irwell where it is crossed by the remarkable Clifton Aqueduct which carried the Manchester, Bolton & Bury Canal over the valley floor. Opened in 1796, it is now a listed heritage structure. Slipping downstream, the route then dives back towards the woods

 and Dam's Head Lodge before arriving at the foot of Prestwich Clough.

The way back is up this thickly wooded vale. It's a very pleasant walk, popular since Edwardian times and which at its peak had tearooms and a bandstand. It's less formal these days; the beautiful woods are now a favourite with nature lovers and birdwatchers, and a network of paths lace the woods, which are part of the Red Rose Forest project established in the 1990s. At the top is the splendid 14th-century St Mary's Church at Prestwich and the adjoining historic old inn.

NOTE: For Public transport, Prestwich Metrolink Station is on the Manchester to Bury line (Tel: Traveline 0871 200 2233)

THE BASICS

Distance: 4 miles / 6.5km
Gradient: Undulating, with several flights of steps
Severity: Moderate
Approximate time: 3 hrs
Stiles: None
Map: OS Explorer 277 (Manchester and Salford)
Path description: Tarred lanes, tracks, woodland paths, pavement; muddy in places
Start point: Prestwich Metrolink Station, Prestwich (GR: SD 813041)
Parking: Car parks at and opposite station (free) (M25 1BP)
Dog friendly: On leads as appropriate (no dogs allowed on Metrolink)
Public toilets: Prestwich shopping centre
Nearest refreshment: Pubs and cafes in Prestwich

PHILIPS PARK WALK

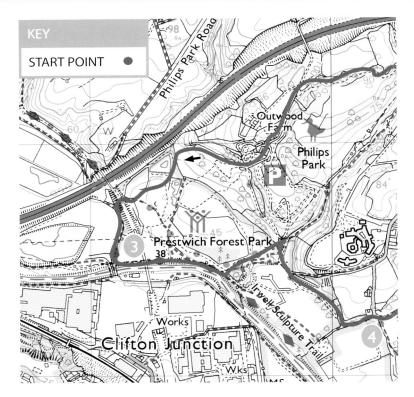

1. Starting from Prestwich Metrolink station (car park side), turn right to Fairfax Road and go left to Bury New Road. Cross into Chester Street, and at the junction go right on Clifton Road. Beyond housing this becomes a tree-lined lane. In 600 yards turn right into Farm Hill (signed Private Road). Past the cottages use the kissing gate and drop through the underpass down to cross the culvert at Bradley Brook.

2. Turn half-left for 10 paces; then right up the stepped path for 'Barn & Gardens', soon bending left through Mid Wood. A meandering stroll through bluebell woods and past ponds reaches a tarred driveway; turn left and fork right in 200 yards to the estate buildings; the mansion was off to your left. Drift right down the tarred lane

beside the conservatory garden, continuing to the far end of the old car park. Take the signed track down to Kingfisher Lodge pond. Below the dam, fork right (not over the footbridge) towards 'Irwell Sculpture Trail (North)'. Use the short tunnel beneath the viaduct, then turn left on the path to reach the river in 400 yards.

3. In front of you is the solid aqueduct that carried the canal over the River Irwell. Turn downstream, soon passing under the viaduct, then over a wide footbridge. In another 300 yards bear left (not sharp left) at the signposted junction along Cycle Route 6 for 'Philips Park'. The track meanders to another major junction at Dam's Head Lodge just past a pylon. Turn right (pond is up on your left) on the track

for Drinkwater Park. At the wood-end barriers in 600 yards turn left up the lane to a sharp left-hand bend in 150 yards.

4. Slip right by the barrier onto the signed path into Prestwich Clough. This enters woodland of beech, oak and lime; at the fork in 250 yards, immediately over the stream, keep ahead up the hollow path, soon rejoining the stream. At the fork before the wide bridge keep right. Cross the next footbridge and stay stream-side, water on your right. Ignore any side paths and bridges, presently reaching wide, shallow steps. At the head of these walk the cobbled pathway to St Mary's churchyard wall. Turn right alongside this to find The Church Inn.

5. Walk up Church Lane to the main road, and cross into the tarred path left of the Red Lion. At its far end turn left up Rectory Lane and wind back to the Metrolink.

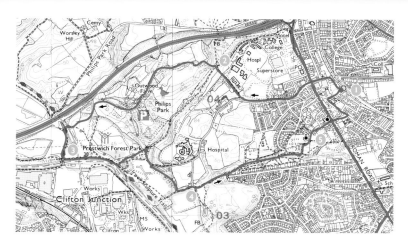

HEALEY DELL

THIS IS AN EXHILARATING RAMBLE BY MOORLAND FRINGE
AND IN A TERRIFIC WOODED GORGE WHERE ROBIN HOOD
ONCE DALLIED.

Just north of Rochdale, the little River Spodden has cut a spectacular gorge deep into the sandstone. It twists and turns from near Whitworth to the outskirts of Rochdale, creating a hidden gem of woodlands and torrents coupled with an intriguing industrial heritage. Paths and tracks criss-cross the vicinity, allowing a great range of rambles to be undertaken. This route sticks to the central part, making the most of the colourful woodlands and secluded hamlets that dapple the edge of the moors.

The spine of the walk is an old railway line. The route between Rochdale, Whitworth and Bacup declined even before the Beeching cuts in the 1960s, losing its passenger services as early as 1947. Much of the trackbed is now a cycleway and footpath, including the spectacular Spodden Viaduct. This leaps across the gorge on eight slender arches 100 feet (30m) above the river's swirling course. There's a giddying view down the gorge and across the thick woodlands that fill it to the surrounding moorland fringes.

The walk starts by threading along old tracks to the weaving and farming hamlets of Prickshaw and Catley Lane Head, huddled below the fringe of the wild moorland. Catley stands at the southern end of the remarkable 'Cotton Famine Road'. This cobbled way across the moors was built in the 1860s by the government-sponsored labour of jobless mill workers, when exports of cotton from the Southern States of America were suspended during the Civil War. It improved a medieval monastic track, now marked by ghostly remains of mines, cottages and a hauliers' pub and followed by the Mary Towneley Loop of the new Pennine Bridleway, which links Middleton in Derbyshire with Kirkby Stephen in Cumbria.

Our route is less challenging; sliding down into peaceful woodland before emerging at the bottom of the gorge and an area of old mills. One of them has a Nature Centre (limited opening) detailing the area's heritage. The final stage of the ramble takes in the view from the old viaduct before exploring the pretty wooded gorge of the Spodden. A few remains of old corn and textile mills; spectacular waterfalls and torrents and legends of fairy folk, witches and Robin Hood tantalise. It's a marvellous final flourish, maybe slippery in places after wet weather, but a remarkable scenic delight at the edge of Rochdale.

*NOTE: Parking at Healey Dell car park is free and is signposted along Station Road, Broadley, off the A671 between Rochdale and Whitworth – turn off the A671 by Healey off licence/shop opposite Tonacliffe Road (at OL12 8SE). For Public transport: Buses from Rochdale, Bacup and Rawtenstall to Broadley (Station Road end); bus 438 from Rochdale to Catley Lane Head (Tel: Traveline 0871 200 2233)

THE BASICS

Distance: 3¼ miles / 5.25km
Gradient: Mostly easy going, with gentle climbs and descents; several sets of steps
Severity: Moderate
Approximate time: 2 to 2½ hrs
Stiles: Several squeeze stiles and gates
Map: OS Explorer OL21 (South Pennines)
Path description: Dirt paths, moorland road, cobbled/tarred lanes, old railway
Start point: Healey Dell Reserve car park (GR: SD 879166)
Parking: Healey Dell car park*
Dog friendly: On leads as appropriate
Public toilets: None
Nearest refreshment: Tea room at Nature Reserve Centre open Fridays to Sundays

HEALEY DELL WALK

1. At the car park, take the stepped path right of the Nature Reserve board, joining the cobbled lane rising past a mill lodge. This soon reaches the houses at Prickshaw; in ruins until 30 years ago. Turn left after Hay Barn, up the Pennine Bridleway for Catley, passing more cottages before easing ahead on the narrow, tarred lane. Keep right beyond the cattle grid at Knacks Farm, up the potholed lane to reach a crossing junction with a wide cobbled track.

2. This is Rooley Moor Road, the Cotton Famine Road. Turn left down this. Beyond the cattle grid at Catley Lane Head turn left on Smallshaw Road.

3. In the near farmyard turn right on the signed footpath through the wide gate then left to a stone gap-stile. Turn right beside the fence, soon entering woodland. At a small clearing in 100 yards drift right, down a good path to cross an old flat bridge; then remain on the path high above the stream. Skirt the left-hand edge of the large grassy clearing, being alert in 30 paces for the path forking left down to a sturdy metal footbridge; cross this and advance by cottage gardens up to a lane.

4. The Nature Reserve Centre is to the right down the rough lane, located in one of the old mill buildings; the tea room is here too. Continue up the woodland lane for another 450 yards to find huge concrete bastions blocking a roadway. Look back-left for the handgate onto a link path up to the old railway. Bear left to reach the viaduct in 1300 yards (1km).

5. Turn back a few paces to use the stepped path left, down to Dell Road. Go left; then in a few yards right, back under the viaduct on a track into the gorge. Evocative remains of the old cotton mill 'Th' Owd Mill i't' Thrutch' straddle the Spodden here. Simply follow

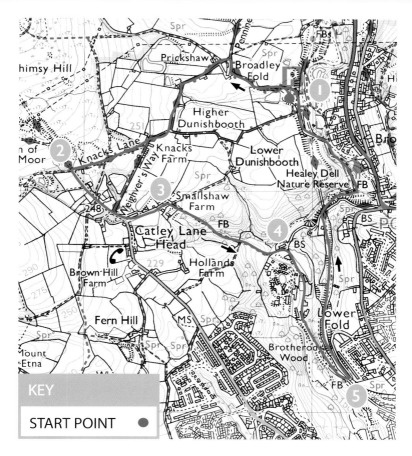

KEY

START POINT ●

the path up the gorge. Near the top a side-path drops to a viewing platform above the Fairies Chapel potholes, where Robin Hood is said to have clashed with a witch and the King of the Fairies! At the top of the main path is Station Road; turn left back to the car park.

CHEESDEN VALLEY

A MOORLAND-EDGE RAMBLE IN THE WEST PENNINES
REVEALING A MAGNIFICENT WOODED GORGE AND
TANTALISING REMAINS OF ABANDONED VILLAGES AND
INDUSTRY.

The large number of wind turbines draping the moorland north of Heywood is simply the latest way to harness energy from natural resources. Skip back a couple of centuries and there was an equally innovative way to make the most of the challenging weather that sweeps across these Pennine Hills.

Water power was the resource exploited from the 1780s onwards. Flowing from the boggy moors, a web of becks has nibbled deeply into the gritstone uplands, creating a series of gorge-like vales. Initially on a small scale, but with increasing complexity as Victorian ingenuity blossomed, the waters flowing to the rivers Roch and Irwell were dammed to power a complex of mills that once employed hundreds.

This walk, the most energetic in this book, explores one of these areas, offering a taste of wilderness and a fascinating heritage well hidden from sight in this magnificent countryside of wooded gulches, rolling hay meadows and memorable views just a short distance from the heart of Bury.

The Cheesden Brook valley contains a remarkable range of remains, from tree-hidden chimneys and wheel-pits to woodland-smothered mills and glistening mill lodges. Starting from a hill village whose mills now house apartments, the walk meanders past farms before joining a field-edge path that skirts the very lip of the gorge – so walk carefully. The thick woods clothing the great bowl at Birtle Dean disguise the site of a huge mill and workers' village which was abandoned over 100 years ago.

Reaching heathery moorland, the short walk turns back to base after a superb wildflower and bird-rich stroll, whilst the longer route (uneven for 200 yards) drops to the valley floor to discover tumbled remains and reed-fringed lakes. An ivy-clad chimney marks the site of Washwheel bleachworks, the last to close hereabouts in 1919. Upstream, cobbled tracks snake to the tumbled remains of the Deeply Vale complex, with ponds, pits and gaunt ruins hidden in the woodland.

From this secluded spot the walk circles back along farm lanes and tracks from which are wide views across Greater Manchester. This longer route is more energetic and has several climbs both up and down. Just take time to enjoy and appreciate the stunning scenery and sense of space here. And there's a good pub at the end to look forward to!

THE BASICS

Distance: 2½ miles / 4km or 5½ miles / 9km

Gradient: Undulating with a few climbs, one short, uneven descent on longer route

Severity: Easy (moderate longer walk)

Approximate time: 2 to 3½ hrs

Stiles: Five (two on short route)

Map: OS Explorer 277 (Manchester and Salford)

Path description: Lanes, field paths, moorland tracks; path is narrow in places and is uneven over tree roots

Start point: Pack Horse Inn, Elbut Lane, Jericho, Bury (GR: SD 835125)

Parking: Roadside above Pack Horse Inn (BL9 7TU)

Dog friendly: On leads through farmland

Public toilets: Facilities at pub for customers

Nearest refreshment: Pack Horse Inn (open all day)

CHEESDEN VALLEY WALK

1. Walk uphill from the Pack Horse, in 440 yards passing Church Lane (left). Take the next right; a narrow lane beside Birtle Grange Farm. Keep left at the fork beyond the bungalow, walking past two farms before approaching a moveable barrier across the descending road.

2. Look left for the waymarked stile and join a path that soon skims the top of woodland. Keep to the field edge; dip through the tip of the clough and continue beyond another stile to a fenced corner. Keep right along the top edge of the woodland fringe at the lip of the Cheesden Gorge. The fence-side path is narrow and uneven in places. Pause frequently to appreciate the vast wooded cleft cleaved into the moorland by glacial meltwaters 13,000 years ago. At the path junction marked by manhole covers, go ahead on the rising fence-side path. The great wooded embayment on your right is Birtle Dean. Stay beside the fence; the path meanders along the gorge-edge then

gradually peels away from the edge and rises beside a wall to reach a sandy lane just below a gate. This is Cuckoo Nar and where the long and short routes part.

3. For the short route, go left through the gate and along the walled track past the mast; then the tarred lane back to the Pack Horse. The longer walk turns right along the sandy track. This bends left, revealing a great panorama of Harcles Hill capped by the Peel Monument. In the valley below-right, a chimneystack rises from the trees; this is your target so, about 50 yards before reaching a bridlegate, drop right on an initially steep and uneven path. Cross two stiles and step over a streamlet; the path presently approaches the chimney, part of the Washwheel bleachworks. About 100 yards before reaching the chimney, fork half-left on a rising, soon partly cobbled track lined with hawthorns. This regains the shoulder of the valley before descending another cobbled road into woodland smothering Deeply Vale Mill's skeletal remains. Cross the dam and turn left on the wide track above the lake. Another reservoir soon appears on your right; the areas of rough ground and tumbled walls mark the site of Deeply Hill village

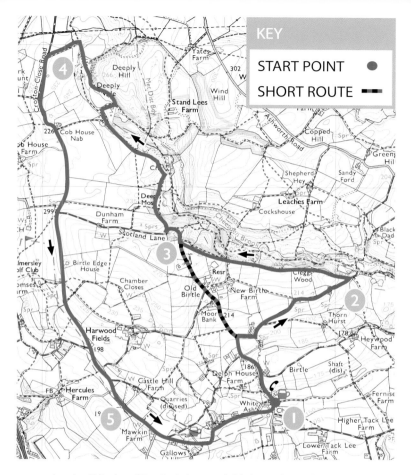

and works. At the top of the short slope turn left below a phone wire, over a gate-side stile and along a cindery track to a gate into a lane.

4. Turn left on the rough lane. Keep left at the junction onto a tarred driveway, fork right at Cob House along the walled bridle path, then advance along the tarred lane beside a golf course.

5. At the sharp-right bend in one mile, turn left (signs for Bircle Church and The Church Inn); then keep ahead, passing the converted school buildings. This roughening track snakes back to the start.

ABOUT THE AUTHOR

Neil Coates' boots have taken him to some of the world's more exotic, far-flung and challenging places. Indian jungles and American canyons; outback deserts and European mountain ranges; remote archipelagos and palm-fringed islets all have a tick next to them, but such lengthy excursions are a rare treat. Much equally appealing terrain lies in England's north-west, and when the chance arises he'll be found exploring the ample countryside of moors and vales, gorges and mosses, shores and woodlands, mountains and watercourses of his native terrain. A keen walker and lover of the countryside since an early age, he's been writing about heritage and countryside locations for many years, combining his work with a close interest in public access to the great outdoors.

A regular contributor to some of the leading outdoor magazines, annual travel and leisure guides and popular book series, he's worked over the years in a variety of jobs in planning, archaeology, countryside management and transport undertakings. Bolton born and Welsh Marches raised, he's spent the last few decades discovering the tracks, byways and paths of the extraordinary landscapes spread lavishly between The Potteries and the Solway Firth, and Shropshire and the windy cliffs of the North Sea coast.

It's the more local countryside where there's so much to discover, however. The long history, industrial heritage and sheer variety of secluded, beautiful and surprising locations within Greater Manchester is one of the great unsung stories of the area. By sharing some of his favourite routes in this book, the hope is that you'll become so hooked on the accessible great outdoors that you'll be keen to make discoveries of your own!